With affection, I dedicate this book to my wife and traveling companion on the Old Gospel Ship

Debra Frost Ramjattan

Her faithfulness and support on the journey has been a source of encouragement to my life and work. Daily our life together has fulfilled Solomon's words:

"Two are better than one, because they have a good reward for their labour." Ecclesiastes 4:9 (KJV)

~

We invite anyone who is interested in helping people experience the fullness of life to partner with us in the development of a four-stage project for the elderly:
Olive's House
(see p. 104)

Donations are welcome.

Contact subesh60@gmail.com
or Oliveshouse2011@gmail.com

NAVIGATING
THE CHALLENGES
OF FAITH-BASED BEHAVIOR

Conduct that exhibits a moral course in life

Subesh Ramjattan, DHL

GREEN WINE™
FAMILY BOOKS

NAVIGATING THE CHALLENGES OF FAITH-BASED BEHAVIOR

Copyright © 2014 by Subesh Ramjattan

Library of Congress Control Number: 2013943818

Ramjattan, Subesh 1951—

Navigating the Challenges of Faith-based Behavior:
Conduct That Exhibits a Moral Course in Life

ISBN 978-1-935434-64-1

Subject Codes and Description: 1: REL 012000: Religion: Christian Life - General 2: REL 012040: Religion: Christian Life - Inspirational 3: RE L012070: Religion: Christian Life – Personal Growth.

Printed in Australia, Brazil, France, Germany, Italy, Spain, UK, and USA

Book Cover Design by Saga Studios Limited, Trinidad and Tobago W. I.

Order from: www.gea-books.com/bookstore/ or subesh60@gmail.com

Published by

GreenWine Family Books

A Division of
GlobalEdAdvancePRESS
www.gea-books.com

CONTENTS

Foreword

This book is truly an admirable and inspiring undertaking by a man who is not only filled with compassion for the less fortunate, but a man who is equally filled with passion and empathy to reach those who do not have a faith-based lifestyle.

The author, Subesh Ramjattan, through the creative analogy of a "Sailing Ship" describes life as a journey that can only be purposeful and fulfilling, if one makes the choice to have a relationship with God. He constantly reminds us of the critical need for guidance and direction along our journey from the Captain of the Ship - Jesus. In reading through the pages of this enthusiastic publication, I therefore could not help but remember and reflect on my own life and purpose and the words which were spoken to me by another entrepreneur, philanthropist and pioneer - Dr. Aleem Mohammed (Chairman of S.M. Jaleel and Company Limited) just a few days before I assumed office as Pro Vice Chancellor and Campus Principal of the UWI St. Augustine Campus. He said, "Whatever your destiny, your challenge is to identify and determine your purpose. Make no mistake about it. We are the children of God. We were created by Him for a particular purpose. We must first seek and understand what that purpose really is. Purposeful work gives meaning and adds value to human life. It goes beyond vision or goal. It's about contributing to the betterment of society and mankind at large." Those thoughts not only still resonate with me about my own purpose and my role in the context of my university, but it also quite aptly describes some of the themes expounded on in this book.

Throughout the thoughtful themes and chapters, Subesh essentially encourages us (the passengers of the Sailing Ship) to take two fundamental steps. The first step is to 'believe' in Jesus Christ (the Captain of the Ship who sets the rules and conduct, and therefore who also has all authority on board). But he does not stop here! Subesh urges us to take a second step, and that is, to 'behave' as Jesus behaved when he walked the earth. He argues that 'behaviour' of a true believer should be marked by a moral lifestyle and therefore should reflect values such as honesty, integrity, loyalty, fairness and goodwill to all men. He calls on all of us to be led by a moral/spiritual compass and to get what he calls our 'moral algebra' correct. And I am a strong proponent that this concept should apply, particularly to leaders across all spheres whether in the public sector, private sector, the church, civil society or universities; leaders of institutions that have influence. This is important because "where the leaders go, the nation follows" as the President of Trinidad and Tobago, His Excellency Anthony Carmona eloquently stated in his Remarks at the Ceremonial Opening of the Fourth Session of the Tenth Parliament of the Republic of Trinidad and Tobago. And so, it is important for our leaders to exhibit strong morals and values and lead by example in every aspect of both personal and professional life. The very nature of their office places them in a responsible position of influence and moral leadership.

But Subesh also goes further to suggest that, "a moral lifestyle also includes an adequate concern for the poor and the disadvantaged." He encourages us therefore to live a life that is greater than ourselves through a spirit of servant-hood. He refers to this as the "plural life", and emphasizes that life is not just about oneself, but rather about others. It indeed reminds me of the words of a great thinker and leader Mahatma Gandhi who once noted that "the best way to find yourself is to lose yourself in the service of others." And this is what true leadership is about, service to others! No one including the poor and needy cares how much you know until you can convince them of how much you care!

The book is replete with relevant scriptures, both from the Old and New Testament which sets foundational truths of life and emphasizes the principles of Christianity. I think Subesh can be confident that there will be many grateful readers who will have gained a broader and practical perspective on how to build a relationship with God, which in turn will ultimately lead us to live more fulfilling, meaningful and purposeful lives. I therefore commend this book as a valuable tool to anyone with an open heart who desires to live, as Subesh writes, "a better life here now and eternal life in the future."

As you read through the pages of this practical and exceptional publication, may you see the inside of the heart of a genuine man of God, a man of compassion and love, and may you be motivated to board the Ship of Zion and stay the course until its final destination!

— **Professor Clement Sankat**
BSc (UWI), MSc (UWI), PhD (Guelph), (Hon.) DLitt (UNB), FIAgrE, CEng. FAPETT
Pro Vice Chancellor and Campus Principal
The University of the West Indies, St. Augustine Campus

Publisher's Preface

There are many comparisons between the old sailing ships and the early songs about the Old Gospel Ship. The sailing ships had rules to secure an adequate crew and safe passage for both ship and cargo. An individual boards the Ship of Zion by invitation, conversion and contract with the Captain. The knowledge-based behavior of Christian converts has similarities with the regulations governing aboard ship conduct and cooperation among the crew. Not only must working sailors know and understand the rules of conduct and operation; they must behave according to the rules or suffer personal consequence and bring great risk to the crew and the ship. This is also true of the faith-based behavior of believers.

The Captain of the ship had total authority aboard a sailing ship and each sailor must follow the guidance of the Captain without question. Failure to follow the rules or obey clear and fixed guidelines created difficult times for all concerned. It was the task of the older crew members to teach, train, and guide the behavior of the younger members. This is also the task of the senior members of the Christian faith. They are responsible to both exhibit and instruct faith-based behavior to the next generation.

There exists a companionship and solidarity of mission among the crew of a sailing ship. Camaraderie among the crew was essential to a safe journey for crew, cargo, and all passengers. There is also an expectation of fellowship and companionship among those who follow Jesus, the Captain of the Old Gospel Ship. This speaks to the company of believers traveling together. They are a "fellowship of believers" traveling together on the same ship. When one individual fails to carry out the proper behavior, other individuals suffer difficulty and the faith-based mission suffers loss. Consequently, the band of believers are accountable to each other and ultimately to the Helmsman of the Ship.

The modern world has lost many of the lessons from the seafaring era. Most social and faith-based leaders are far from the seafaring age and the concept of "helmsman" escapes their vocabulary. There are many definitions of cybernetics and this is a problem for a faith-based understanding. The original intent of the word is lost in the input of various ideas into working definitions to fit a particular personal field of interest. Cybernetics treats not things but ways of behaving. It does not ask "what is this thing?" but "what does it do?" and "what can it do?" An understanding of this definition would bring us back to the original intent of cybernetics: "a helmsman who steers the ship." Modern man has imposed multiple definitions on many words that have value to people of faith. That is the reason for structuring this book around a sailing ship in the seafaring era to review the process of getting crew and cargo to a safe harbor.

The term "helmsman" comes from the Greek word, kybernētēs, and is translated as "cybernetics" which misses the original meaning of steering a ship. The helmsman was the one who guided the course of the ship and understood both the workings of the ship, the currents, the winds, and the nature of the waters in which the ship was sailing. The Helmsman of the Old Gospel Ship is clearly Jesus and those who presume to follow His leadership must accept as His words of **invitation** and faithfully follow the written guidance in the preserved Sacred Writings.

With these concepts and constructs in mind, those who accept the **invitation** to board the Ship of Zion are **converted** from their old life and established in a moral lifestyle. Lifestyle is a word from sociology meaning the way a person lives; it suggests a style of living that reflects the attitudes and values of a person. To establish a moral lifestyle one must both **believe** and **behave** the clear concepts presented in the preserved Sacred Writings. This lifestyle both honors the historical past and changes those who observe the proper conduct of believers. Change comes to others when they encounter the fervent witness of those blessed by the power of a divine invitation.

> 27. While He spoke, a woman in the crowd, with a loud voice said, Blessed is the Mother who birthed you and nursed you .28. But Jesus said, Rather blessed are those who hear the word of God and behave it (Luke 11:27-28 EDNT).

The sailing guidelines passed on by skilled seamen and officers became a **working contract** for new seamen to keep the ship afloat and the crew safe. The crew of a sailing ship beside the officers included: cabin boys sent to sea to learn the ropes and the maritime trade and carpenters who kept the ship afloat and made necessary repairs. Good crew members were of great value to a sailing ship. This is equally true of individuals whose faith-based **contract** places them in a responsible position of moral leadership and faithful service for the benefit of others.

The lack of moral lifestyle among some in faith-based groups is troubling. Bad behavior diminishes the testimony of the faithful, as much as, a leak below the water line of a ship. Being a part of the fellowship of believers requires everyone to follow the rules. When anyone fails in this area of responsibility, the whole community suffers. This is similar to a crew member of a sailing ship failing to perform vital duties that endangers the ship, the cargo and the crew.

Normally, a new believer is willing to follow the rules and the spiritual guidance of a respected leader. An example of this behavior is a new convert in Hong Kong who wrote his mother in mainland China "I am now reading the Bible and **behaving** it." He had the right idea. Conversion is supposed to regenerate the soul and redirect the priorities of daily life. According to Scripture, conversion is to produce a new creation that generates a revitalized soul that brings into being a moral witness. We need more converts who **read, believe and clearly behave preserved Sacred Writings**.

The Sacred Covenant charts a course of action to guide believers on their journey from earth to heaven. It is not necessary to search for a route or worry about the next phase of the journey. With confidence in the Helmsman of the Ship, and the fellowship of other believers, it is just a matter of following the rules and accepting spiritual guidance. Sure there will be challenges along the way, temptations will come that must be resisted, choices must be made, and other circumstances that could push one off course, but those difficulties can be dealt with through simple faith and trust. When one has trust in God and a covenant alliance with other believers, the behavior for the journey should be clear. Each thought and act should move one closer to faith and forward toward the ultimate goal – a moral lifestyle. A faith-based lifestyle determines both the course of action, the destination of the journey and provides a standard of behavior appropriate for one traveling on the Old Gospel Ship. Come join Subesh Ramjattan on the Ship of Zion sailing toward the eternal shores of Paradise.

— The Publisher

Author's Introduction

When I see friends who do not have a faith-based lifestyle, my heart is troubled. I constantly wonder, "What can I do to share with them the true joy of living a faith-based life?" I see each opportunity as an obligation to share my Christian witness. I hope that my friends will see my sincerity and observe the joy that Debbie and I have in serving Jesus and traveling as active crew members on the Old Gospel Ship. This book is part of my effort to reach colleagues, family and friends with guidance for the faith-based behavior that leads to a better life here and now and eternal life in the future. **"Welcome friends! Come aboard, travel with me on the Ship of Zion."**

As I see others who profess to be believers but have no active witness to share their faith, I am disappointed to say the least. Some of my friends have such an insecure relationship with God, they appear similar to the man standing with a rope in his hand wondering, **"Did I find a rope or did I lose my horse?"** They profess a faith in God, but stand idle without a standard of living that is marked by an active witness or moral lifestyle. It appears that some simply follow the crowd, copy the actions of others, and participate in the same activities without understanding the value of a faith-based way of life. They observe a spiritual sailor tie a special knot in a special rope to bring security to the ship, but do not understand the reason for the knot or the necessity of the specific behavior. I am not speaking of personal appearance, but of attitude and a limited capacity to grasp the grace of spiritual behavior and become a responsible and moral witness to God's love and eternal blessings available to all.

> 3. **Do you think that you will escape the condemnation of God that do the same things you criticize others for doing?** 4. Or do you entertain wrong ideas about God's truce, His kindness and longsuffering; not knowing that the kindness of God causes you to turn away from evil and begin a new moral life? (Romans 2:3-4 EDNT)

There is a story about a rural church that decided to ask the farmers in the congregation to select a calf in their herd and raise it for missions. It seems that when the time came to sell the "fatted calf" and present the money to the church for missions, one farmer decided the young calf was just too good to sell for missions. He decided to keep the calf and give the church an amount less than the market value of the calf. As he approached the church with the "limited offering," his conscience began to nag at him about his plans to deceive the church. As he walked up the steps to the front door, the choir was singing about the glory of God and the song had a line *"The half has never been told."* What the farmer's guilty conscience heard was **"The calf has never been sold."** This prodded the farmer to confess and pledge to provide the full value of the calf. It appears difficult to hide wrongdoing and the best way to deal with moral deficiency is to permit God to work a spiritual change in both the soul and the behavior.

The story about the unsold calf presents the fact that believers must make a continuing commitment to a faith-based lifestyle and never attempt to limit what is due the Lord's work. Malachi presented this question "Will a man rob

God?" The clear answer was "in tithes and offerings." (Malachi 3:8) The Tithe is ten percent of personal earnings, but the worth of an offering relates to what the giver has left. In other words, an offering is measured by what it cost the giver, not the actual value of the gift. The comment of Jesus about the small gift of a widow, "She has given more than you all," speaks to the value of her gift.

Some who fail in the matter of money also deprive the fellowship of their energy, time and the moral witness of a faith-based lifestyle. The neglect of money matters often spills over into the spiritual and social aspects of life. The true joy of giving is lost and the rewards of service to God and others are missing. A moral lifestyle includes an adequate concern for the poor and the disadvantaged. When one's eyes become accustomed to the darkness of neglect, much of the joy of life is misplaced. Perhaps, we should also tithe our time, talent, and targeted efforts for the disadvantaged.

> 4 ...Lord, when did we see you hungry, or athirst, or homeless, or naked, or sick, or in prison, and did not minister to you? 45. Then will He answer, saying, Truly, I say, Inasmuch as you did not serve one of the least of these, you did it not to Me. (Matthew 25:44b - 45 EDNT)

Has anyone said lately, "You light up my life?" A romantic ballad written by Joe Brooks, but turned into an inspirational hit by Debbie Boone has some words relevant to this book:

> *Rolling at sea, Adrift on the waters.*
> *Could it be finally I'm turning for home?*
> *And you Light up my life. You give me hope to carry on.*
> *You light up my days, and fill my nights-- with song.*

Jesus spoke of John the Disciple and said, "he was a burning fire in a shinning lamp: and you were pleased to walk in his light" (John 5:35 EDNT). The darker the night the brighter your light will shine. Some say the light of a single candle in total darkness shines all the way to the moon, 217,000 miles away. This means even a small light can light up the lives of those around you. You can give others hope. Just let your light shine. Matthew recorded the words of Jesus, "Let your light shine so others can see your good works and glorify your Father, who is in Heaven." Jesus expects His followers to shine light on the pathway of others so they can find their way to boarding dock the Old Gospel Ship.

> 33. No man who lights a lamp puts it in a closet, nor under a box, but on a lamp stand so all may see the light. 34. The lamp of the body is the eye: therefore, when your eye is focused your whole body has light; but when your eye is morally bad, your body is full of darkness. 35. Take care that the reflected light in you does not come from moral darkness. 36. **If you have light for the body with the absence of darkness, the whole shall be light, as when a candle shines brightly in the dark** (Luke 11:33-36 EDNT).

I have met some "almost disciples" who were like the farmer on a slow wind day, who tore down one of his two windmills because he thought there wasn't enough wind to turn them both. There is always sufficient wind of the Spirit to refresh all believers willing to work in the kingdom and assist the less fortunate. Some without basic knowledge of the scripture, ask God to make room for them in **heaven** when there is no room for God in their **heart** and no **place** in their lifestyle for the needy of their community. Such folk are looking for a relocation plan and eternal fire insurance and not a way of life. This is not what salvation is about; eternal life is a blood covenant with God. It is serious business; Jesus shed His blood to save and bring eternal life to those who believe. According to the Sacred Writings, "The poor hear the gospel gladly." Assisting the less fortunate is part of a faith-based lifestyle. It is also true that the "up and out" as well as the "down and out" need to hear the good news. This is the essence to a faith-based life of witness to others.

In ancient times, God had a plan to save the obedient during the Great Flood. He instructed Noah to build an Ark to save those who would believe the flood was coming and would willingly enter the safety of the Ark. Yet, most individuals demonstrated the normal human skepticism about ultimate redemption. They refused to believe. In the New Testament, Jesus constructed the Old Gospel Ship to transport people of faith to the shores of Heaven. Still, many refuse to accept the divine deliverance and free transportation to God's Paradise.

One must choose to board the Old Gospel Ship on God's terms, or lose their free ticket on the Old Gospel Ship; God is not a backup plan for lazy, "almost disciples of Jesus" who associate with religious groups only for personal gain and not for personal salvation or moral service. Some call such distant followers, "in-laws to the church" they may have a good companion, but personally they follow at a distance.

> **Love does not intentionally do wrong** to a neighbor: love, therefore, satisfies the law completely. 11. The time is now that you must awake to reality: for salvation is nearer that when we first believed. 12. The night is almost over and dawn is near: let us therefore lay aside the clothing of the night, and put on the weapons of light. 13. **Let us behave honestly in the day light**; not in partying and intoxicated behavior, not in secret places of immorality, not in conflict and greed. 14. **But clothe yourselves with the Lord Jesus Christ,** and make no plans to fulfill the desires of the flesh (Romans 13:10-14 EDNT).

The purpose of this book is to encourage my friends to make a faith-based commitment and scriptural connection with Jesus and other believers. The seafaring theme is to assist both the faith and the behavior of those who would follow Christ. It is my hope that my family, friends, and colleagues will follow Christ with enthusiasm. The original meaning of the word "enthusiasm" was behavior inspired by God. This is what I desire for Navigating the Challenges of Faith-based Behavior.

The design of this book is to present the **behavior** of followers of Christ in a nautical/sailing ship framework to illustrate the struggle of some to both **believe** (have confidence in the Sacred Writings) and **behave** (conduct themselves in an established lifestyle of witness to others). I will have fulfilled my purpose if others develop a moral lifestyle and follow Jesus with a warm heart and witness with enthusiasm about the blessings of a lifestyle based on faith.

Debbie and I invite friends and family to come aboard and travel with us on the magnificent journey that includes a good life on earth and eternal life in the Paradise of God. Come journey with us, the best is yet to be! Come aboard, travel with us on the Ship of Zion." --Subesh Ramjattan

---

Most references in this book are from the EVERGREEN Devotional New Testament (EDNT) of which Debbie and I were Patrons to assist the publication. You may obtain a copy of the EDNT by ordering it from www.gea-books. com or subesh60@gmail.com. ISBN 978-1-9354349-26-9. Complete Edition 2014. It is also available where good books are sold.

CHAPTER ONE

Charting a Course

*I have good news to bring
And that is why I sing,
All my joys with you I will share.
Well I'm gonna take a trip
On the old gospel ship
And go sailing through the air.*

— Stamps-Baxter

Charting a Life Course

Some wait too late to map out their course for life. The value of a charted course relates to both the terminal objective and the time one has to travel toward stated goals. The reasonable thing to do would be to plan a course for life early and permit the ultimate objective to guide your forward steps. If one fails to establish adequate life goals, personal and professional challenges could blot out the normal opportunities to advance the agenda for their life.

God Has a Plan

Life is not a voyage to nowhere! God has a plan for each life. From the foundation of the world, God planned a way forward for each member of the human race. Although individuals and groups of people have strayed from the Right Path, God will always send someone to guide those who seek the path of truth. The Jewish Fathers say that each person who has or will ever live on earth is in the code of the Torah and that God mapped out their life before the foundation of the world. Some may question this possibility but according to Saint Peter, "The Lord is not slow concerning His promise as some count slowness; but is longsuffering to all, not wishing any to perish, but desiring all to take the way of repentance (2 Peter 3:9 EDNT). This opens the door for all.

The Right Path

When the ancient scripture recorded "Redeem the time because the days are evil," (Ephesians 5:16), it clearly spoke directly to how the evils of daily life could rob one of the opportunity to follow the Right Path. There is a different rendering of this verse in the Devotional New Testament, "Buying up every opportunity, because these are evil days," this suggests there is a cost to take advantage of an opportunity, as it is available. The ancient record shows that the Prophet Muhammad predicted that people would lose their way and "Allah would send another messenger to guide them back to the right path." The good news is that many years ago a man, known as Jesus, sacrificed His life to purchase eternal salvation for the whole world. Consequently, each individual has a free pass to a new and better way of life for the present and better life after death. The only obligation when accepting the free-gift of salvation is a promise to travel on the Right Path and develop a moral lifestyle worthy of eternal life in Paradise.

A Choice or a Chance

Normally, we fix attention on only one cross, but those who viewed the scene at Calvary saw three crosses. Malice had placed Jesus between two thieves. In some respects, the three men were alike: their time on earth was limited and they were in the process of dying. From the middle cross, one learns a lesson about forgiveness rather than rebellion. One man was **dying for sin** on a cross of redemption. On another cross, a man was **dying in sin** on a cross of rebellion and rejection. On the other cross, a man was **dying freed from sin** on a cross of repentance. There were three men, each on a cross, but not all dying the same way or for the same reason. In the context of their present situation, each man was choosing the nature and destination for their afterlife. Each had a choice of reincarnation of the soul before death with assurance of eternal life in Paradise or "take a chance" and face the unknown region of the dead without redemptive assurance. It is simply a choice or a chance. Most reasonable individuals would choose the saving assurance of eternal life.

The Cross of Redemption has meaning when one views the crucifixion through the open tomb of the resurrection and sees an empty cross. Jesus was the substitute for the sins of mankind; His cross was the means of redemption and reconciliation with God. His resurrection validated God's plan to save those who believe. Only when one believes and daily walks in fellowship with the risen Christ can they truly realize the value of Calvary. Jesus paid the price for the sins of the human race and made redemption available to those who both personally believe and behave the lifestyle Jesus established. Following Jesus produces a moral lifestyle easily seen by all who dare to observe the disciples of Jesus. This unknown statement, **"It takes more nails to close a wooden coffin than it took to nail Jesus to the Cross,"** exemplifies the willingness of Christ to sacrifice His life for the salvation of the world. The wonderful thing about the Cross of Redemption is that Jesus died for everyone who will humbly ask forgiveness for past sins and claim the saving assurance of eternal life.

On the Cross of Rebellion and Rejection, one sees a man who lived as a thief and died as a thief. His rebellious attitude toward Jesus was present in the hour of his death. It is a mystery how this Jewish man came to such a desperate end. He was bitter, rebellious even in the presence of the tenderness of Jesus who said, "Father, forgive them for they know not what they do." This man simply did not have the personal "faith" taught by the Prophets. He obviously knew that a Messiah was coming, but came to Jesus with doubt asking, **"If you are the Son of God, save yourself and us?"** The vagueness of his request signaled a desire to escape imminent death, but with no intention of making personal changes and developing a different lifestyle. Christ did not promise to save people from the difficult crosses of human existence; He promised a better life with hope for the future that included eternal life. Yet this thief attempted to dictate the terms of his "saving." One who seeks redemption is saved to serve God in the real world of human difficulties, not just to escape punishment for sin. Sadly, many today still attempt to dictate the terms of their salvation and try to barter with God. In doing so, they miss the greatest bargain of all, free redemption that comes with simple faith in Christ.

On the Cross of Repentance, one sees a man who knew he was a thief and was being justly punished. Perhaps in his dying hour he began to see things in a new light. He witnessed some of the persecution Jesus received from the people, yet he saw in Jesus a humble individual who forgave others. He saw and heard the unjust harassment of Jesus by the other thief. He saw the tenderness of Jesus, and freely admitted his sins and asked for mercy. He made no demands just **"Lord, remember me when you come into your kingdom."** Recognizing that Christ was the Lord of the future, he wanted to be worthy to be part of His Kingdom. He found repentance, redemption, and mercy. Hearing the words **"Today, you will be with me in Paradise"** was both deliverance and reassurance, together with eternal life in the presence of Jesus, the Christ. This was not deliverance from the just punishment of wrongdoing in society, but redemption of the soul and the promise of eternal life in Paradise. This was the best day of his life; it was the end of his suffering and fear about the afterlife. He had saving assurance of life after death with Jesus in Paradise.

> 39. One of the crucified wrongdoers began to behave in an irresponsible way, saying, If you are Christ, save yourself and us. 40. But the other scolded him, saying, Do you not fear God, seeing you are under a guilty verdict? 41. And we indeed receive just punishment for our deeds: but this man has done nothing wrong. 42. And he said to Jesus, **Lord, remember me when you come into your kingdom.** 43. And Jesus answered, Truly I say, **Today you will be with Me in paradise.** (Luke 23:39-43 EDNT)

> *The dying thief rejoiced to see*
> *That fountain in his day,*
> *And there may I, as vile as he*
> *Wash all my sins away.*

> — William Cowper (1731–1800)
> *There Is a Fountain*

So Near Yet so Far

Jesus said, "If I be lifted up, I will draw all men unto me." In response to his humble cry of faith, the dying thief became the only recorded deathbed repentance and conversion. Only one example of God's Grace so none would despair, but only one so none would presume. By faith, the urgent request from one thief for a place in the kingdom of Christ was answered. A free ticket for the same day on the Old Gospel Ship to Paradise was his. The ticket was marked **"For immediate boarding."** Another thief was lost in the sea despair because of rejection and un-forgiven sins. He was so near the Savior, but so far from redemption across the great fixed gulf of unbelief. Reproved by his colleague in crime, but not redeemed by the Christ of Calvary. His ticket purchased by Christ for the Old Gospel Ship was never picked-up and validated. It was not lost, but it was not transferable; it was available to the thief only on request. Yet, anger and doubt in the confusion of crucifixion caused him to stubbornly refuse redemption.

Access to the Ship of Faith

The thief who asked for mercy illustrates four steps to receive access to the Ship of Faith; they are **attention, interest, desire,** and **action**. These steps are obvious in the case of the penitent thief.

Attention: his arrest and sentence of death by crucifixion certainly did grab his attention. The act of observing Jesus being nailed to the cross and witnessing the ranting of his fellow thief against Jesus, certainly did claim the awareness of his plight and brought increased interest in eternal salvation.

Interest: the enraged outcry against Jesus and the words "save yourself and us" created an interest in the possibility of deliverance. This interest in present and future salvation created a desire to seek the possibility of a place in Christ's kingdom.

Desire: the possibility of being a part of the future Kingdom of Christ created a willingness to seek mercy from the middle cross. The action was clearly a desire for "life after death" in the Paradise of God.

Action: the engagement of the other thief in a verbal reprimand declaring the innocence of Jesus opened the door. Seeing Jesus, as a Person of authority and passion, created the opportunity for the request "Lord, remember me when you come into your kingdom." The use of "Lord" and "Kingdom" together with the personal pronoun "me" prompted an immediate response, "Today, you will be with Me in Paradise." This was total redemption for the man and a promise of a blessed future: the words "today" and "paradise" were greater mercy than expected, but not more than the Crucified Christ promises to all who ask in faith for a place in His kingdom. The recording of these facts in scripture provides the hope of salvation for all who will chart the same course of action. Since redemption and paradise are available to all, the message of grace and mercy is open to everyone by a simple act of faith.

The wise man Solomon in his autobiography was concerned about an empty life without permanent value that leads to frustration. He wrote, **"Pursue your course but know that God will judge your behavior."** (Ecclesiastes 11.9 DOT) The fact that we must give account for wrongdoing brings to mind the story of a summer camp director who was explaining the beauty of nature and concluded "God created all things for the benefit of the people." At this, a nine-year-old boy with an arm covered with calamine lotion asked, "Why did God make poison ivy?" Before the director could come up with a brilliant theological answer about the fall of Adam and Eve that brought thorns and thistles to the earth, another boy spoke up "That was to teach us to keep our hands off some things." Yes, true discipleship requires one to deny wrong attitudes and actions to develop a moral lifestyle of witness for Jesus. Lifestyle discipleship includes **being, believing, becoming,** and **behaving.**

Being is at the core of human behavior; it stems from knowing yourself and becomes the essence of who you are. Being answers the question "Why do I exist?" The first question in the historic Westminster Catechism (1647) read:

Q. What is the chief end of man?
A. Man's chief end is to glorify God, and to enjoy Him
   forever.

The purpose of God, in creating the human race, is clearly understood, not by a study of theology, but by the story of a godly mother, putting her daughter to bed. The mother asked the first question of the Catechism and received the normal answer. Then the mother without quite realizing why, asked, "And what do you think is the chief end of God?" Thinking a moment, the child answered wisely: **"Since the chief end of Man is to glorify God and enjoy Him forever, then the chief end of God must be to glorify Man and enjoy him forever."** Without the knowledge of philosophy that the converse of a proposition is also true, the child profoundly answered the question. Everything we know about God and Creation affirms the wisdom of the child's answer. It is God's desire to have fellowship with redeemed human beings through the redemptive work of Jesus.

A Right Standing with God

> 17. Therefore if any man be in Christ, he is a new creation: observe, the old things have passed away; all things have become new. 18. All things are of God, who has brought us together in Himself by Jesus Christ, and has given to us the ministry of bringing people together; 19. how that God was in Christ bringing together the world to Himself, not counting their false steps and blunders against them; and has committed us to speak intelligent words that bring man and God together. 20. Now seeing we are representatives for Christ, as though God did make His appeal through us: we implore you in Christ's stead, come together with God. 21. **For God caused Christ to become sin for us, who knew no sin; that we might come into right standing with God in Christ** (2 Corinthians 5:17-21 EDNT).

Believing is the most important step toward salvation, but believing is not enough. It must be right believing and acceptance of the underpinning of a spiritual sense of certainty. Believing requires accepting as true a firm faith in God and His plan for one's life. One must believe that Jesus is the Son of God and that His Crucifixion was to redeem the world. Faith "in" is not sufficient; there must be faith "on." The difference with "in and on" is best illustrated with the story of the early elevator. When a man approached an elevator for the first time, he refused to walk onboard. In the early days each elevator had an operator, the operator asked the man "Do you not believe in elevators?" The answer was, "Yes, I believe in elevators; I believe they go up and down." The operator responded, "Why not take a ride on the elevator?" With an anxious voice, the man replied, "I believe **in** elevators that they exist, but I don't trust elevators and can't believe **on** an elevator." There must be trust in the message of grace before one is willing to step onto the Ship of Faith. One must

accept as true the redemptive words of Jesus and the witness
of His followers and be willing to take the step of faith that
places them on the Old Gospel Ship.

> 10. **that you might behave worthy of the pleasing of
> the Lord, personally bearing good fruit and increasing
> in the full knowledge of God;** 11. being empowered
> according to His glorious power, with a cheerful exercise of
> endurance and unlimited perseverance; 12. joyously giving
> thanks to the Father, who made us sufficient to partake of
> the inheritance of the saints who live in the light: 13. who
> has rescued us from the dominion of darkness, and has
> transformed us into the kingdom of His dear Son: 14. **In
> whom we have redemption through His blood, even
> the forgiveness of sins:** (Colossians 1:10-14 EDNT)

Becoming is the process of growing into a mature state
and requires changing and developing into something more
than what you were before. All living things have a time of
becoming; for example, infancy, puberty, formative period, a
growing period, a maturing, and growing older. These phases
are also true of a new believer or convert to Christianity.
What kind of person are you becoming personally and
spiritually? Each one is first a self-aware being, then a
believing person, and then there is a time of becoming who
and what they are to be. It is a time of learning to believe,
learning to trust, and learning to walk the Jesus way.   Even
the Child Jesus had a period of growth and development. He
developed mentally, physically, spiritually, and socially. (Luke
2:52) Note the order of development: the mind, the body, the
spirit, and only then do we develop the social aspects of life.
Most want to put social before spiritual; that is, favor with
man before favor with God. This is not the example of the
Child Jesus.

Behaving is the way individuals conduct themselves
during and following the becoming phase. Doing right
and feeling right are related. How do individuals conduct
themselves? The behaving phase of life has two half-circles.
With this in mind, we can examine **the full circle of human**

experience and relationship. The starting point is the **individual**. A person thinks either of himself or of others.

In the first half-circle, an individual experiences the world as an individual and thinks of self in terms of others and this predisposition is determined by the level of maturity. In this part of the circle, individuals usually use others for personal advantage. Without regard for the privileges and rights of others, they think only of personal desires or goals. The "we" of joint activity is probably a self-aggrandizing "I" and does not mean much. The leader may take credit of a corporate task with no mention of those who actually did the work. An officer may receive the laurels of victory, when in fact it was the foot soldiers who actually fought and won the battle. In this first half-circle, everything seems to revolve around the individual.

In the second half-circle, an individual's experience relates more to others than to self. The essence of being is not in the individual alone, but in interpersonal relationships. Such connection with others can only be found when individuals freely associate with others at the spiritual level. Proper relationship with others is essential to a meaningful human experience. When a person accepts restoration to fellowship with God through Jesus Christ, that individual must involve others in their life. One naturally becomes concerned with the needs and desires of others. When one walks with Jesus, there is an unending search for a satisfying relationship with everyone along the way.

> 17. Whereas the wisdom that comes from above is marked by purity, then peacefulness; it is courteous and ready to be convinced, always taking the better part, It carries mercy with it and is a harvest of all that is good, undivided in mind, without hypocrisy. 18. Peace is the seed-ground of righteousness, and those who make peace will reap the harvest. (James 3:17 EDNT)

Walking in the will of God brings people into positive contact with others. Those who follow Jesus are certain their behavior measures up to faith-based standards. Living in harmony with others, assisting them, being a good example is the moral minimum for the true believer. A joint believer encounter, as spokes in a wheel, forms the support of "togetherness" and constructs the wheel of spiritual completeness that moves one forward in faith and practice. Walking by faith makes one live a plural life as demonstrated in the Prayer the Lord taught His Disciples: "**Our** Father…Give **us**…forgive **us**…as **we** forgive…lead **us**… deliver **us**…" The spiritual life is a plural life; it is living a life greater than yourself. It is a coming together in one mind and in one accord to worship **the One and only God Creator and Sustainer of the Universe.** "Where two or three are gathered **together**, there am I in the midst." Together is the operative word. If we want Jesus to be a part of our family and attend our worship, we must be **together** in unity.

THE LORD'S PRAYER

Our Father who art in heaven, hallowed be Thy name.
Thy kingdom come, Thy will be done, on earth as it is in heaven.
Give us this day our daily bread and forgive us our trespasses as
we forgive those who trespass against us, and lead us not into
temptation, but deliver us from evil.
For Thine is the kingdom and the power and the glory
Now and forever , Amen…

Lifestyle Witness

In the arena of spirituality, lifestyle is the strategic inner compass that guides both attitude and behavior. Self-image is a controlling factor in the way one behaves. Lifestyle provides intentionality to conduct and enables one to behave in a planned and deliberate way. Christian conversion brings regeneration to the soul and redirects the heart in the direction of moral goodness. It is the way one lives daily, that produces their Christian witness. In fact, the word "witness" in the Greek is martyr. This concept was only for the faithful few who gave their life as a witness for Christ. They were not a martyr because they died; they died because of the way they lived. Their life was a witness for Christ and death by various means caused others to classify them as a Martyr. The Book of Hebrews recorded the lives and death of faithful men and women, who traveled the way of faith and lived a life that often brought them death. All believers have "a great crowd of witnesses" looking over the battlements of heaven to observe their behavior. Knowing that others lived the Christian life to the fullest is a source of encouragement of a life of moral witness.

The Witness of Martyrs

The martyrdom of Polycarp, a celebrated figure in the Church history, stands as one of the most well documented events of antiquity. Rome unleashed attacks against Christians during this period, and members of the early church recorded many of the persecutions and deaths. Rome considered Christianity a dangerous cult; therefore, Polycarp placed under arrest on the charge of being a Christian was among an angry mob. The Roman proconsul took pity on such a gentle old man and urged Polycarp to proclaim, "Caesar is Lord." If only Polycarp would make this declaration and offer a small pinch of incense to Caesar's statue he would escape torture and death. To this Polycarp responded, "Eighty-six years I have served Christ, and He never did me any wrong. How can I blaspheme my King who saved me?" Steadfast in his stand for Christ, Polycarp refused to compromise his beliefs and was bound and burned at the stake, then stabbed when the fire failed to reach him in time to satisfy the crowd. Many have died for what they believe, but none died for a lie. Polycarp, and other martyrs, died for Christ because as believers they lived for Christ. Should any doubt the facts of martyrdom, they should read Foxe's Book of Martyrs and examine the biblical text in light of the willful deaths of nearly all of its writers (Hebrews 11: 32-12:17), men who were eyewitnesses to the life and ministry of Christ.

Men of whom the world was not worthy

32. And what more shall I say? Time will fail me to recount the story of Gideon, Barak, Samson, Jephthah, David, Samuel and of the prophets, 33. men who, through faith, mastered kingdoms, did righteousness, obtained promises, shut the mouths of lions. 34. Quenched the power of fire, escaped the edge of the sword, in their weakness they were made strong, showed courage in battle, made foreign armies yield. 35. There were women who received their dead children back to life: and others were tortured, not accepting deliverance; looking forward to a better resurrection: 36. And others experienced mockery and scourging, chains and imprisonment; 37. they were stoned, they were cut in pieces, they were tortured, they were slain with the sword; they wandered about, dressed in animal skins; being destitute, afflicted, tormented; 38. men of whom the world was not worthy: they wandered in desert places, and in mountains, and lived in caves and holes in the earth. 39. And these all, having obtained a good report through faith, received not the promise: 40. For us, God had something better in store. We were needed, to make the history of their lives complete. (Hebrews 11:32-40 EDNT)

Life is full of personal performance, group activities, and individual deeds in various relationships. Lifestyle has to do with the daily routine of everyday life. Lifestyle suggests a standard of living and a level of influence witnessed by the public. It clearly reveals to others the course of action that individuals have charted for themselves. The guidelines in the Scripture must become a true compass to direct the path a believer walks. The record of two disciples on the road to Emmaus following the Crucifixion of Christ points to the fact that Jesus walks with His disciples whether they recognize the fact or not.

14. Their conversation was about all the things that had happened. 15. While they were discussing the whole matter, **Jesus Himself overtook them and walked beside them.** 16. For some reason their eyes did not

recognize Him. 17. And Jesus asked, What are you talking about as you walk that makes you so sad? 18. Cleopas answered, Are you a stranger in Jerusalem, and do not know the things that happened in the past few days? 19. He asked, What things? They answered, Concerning Jesus of Nazareth, who was a mighty prophet in word and deed before God and all the people: 20. and how the high priests and our leaders delivered Him to be sentenced to death and be crucified. 21. We had confidence that He was the one who would redeem Israel: and three days have passed since this happened. (Luke 24:14-21 EDNT)

> *I was standing on the banks of the river*
> *Looking out over life's troubled sea*
> *When I saw that ole ship that was sailing*
> *Is that the ole ship of Zion I see.*
> *Its hull was bent and battered*
> *From the storms of life I could see*
> *Waves were rough but that ole ship kept sailing*
> *Is that the ole ship of Zion I see.*
>
> *At the stern of the ship stood the captain*
> *I could hear as he called out my name*
> *Get on board it's the ole ship of Zion*
> *It will never pass this way again*
>
> *As I step on board I'll be leaving*
> *All my sorrows and heartaches behind*
> *I'll be safe with Jesus the captain*
> *Sailing out on the ole ship of Zion.*
>
> — M. J. Cartwright

Several hymns about ships became popular many years ago in religious services. The image of Christianity as a vessel sailing from earth to heaven with a crew of the faithful was a perennial favorite, occurring in both old hymns and modern songs. It is one of the best-known themes of the best-loved spiritual hymns.

CHAPTER TWO

Boarding the Ship

Come, hoist the sail, the fast let go!
They're seated all aboard.
Wave chases wave in easy flow:
The bay is fair and broad.

(Verse from The Pleasure Boat by Richard Henry Dana)

The Ticket is Free

There is no charge to board the Old Gospel Ship, but there are requirements to qualify for a ticket. A remorseful attitude for past misdeeds and a true, spiritual conversion experience that alters behavior are required. When the requirement is met, an individual is considered a born again believer walking in fellowship with the Lord. This experience puts an individual in close association with others on the journey of faith. There is also an expectation: one who is a true believer will share faith-based principles with family, friends, and other colleagues in the marketplace. In other words, a true believer will have an active lifestyle established by faith-based behavior and will joyfully share the experience of personal redemption with others. Why, because a true believer wants family, friends and colleagues to board the Ship of Faith for the spiritual journey to a better life and a Safe Harbor at journey's end.

Rules of the Ship

There are always rules for any worthy endeavor. The death of Christ defined the essential quality of a moral life based on the principles of love and the rule of right conduct. The concept of moral behavior issues out of the love of Jesus; this love produces right conduct by those who follow Jesus. It is a moral law and the central theme of the teachings of

Jesus. He taught that the heart was the seat of all virtue and the spring of all faith-based behavior. Jesus said, "What is impossible with man, is possible with God." (Luke 18:27) Redemption for all may seem an impossible task, but no one is far from the Kingdom.

> 28. And one of the scribes came, and having heard the discussion, perceived that Jesus had answered admirably, asked, Which of the commandments is in first position? 29. And Jesus answered, The chief one is, Hear, O Israel; The Lord your God is one Lord: 30. And thou shall love the Lord your God with your whole heart, and with your whole existence, and with all your moral understanding, and with all your ability and strength: 31. namely this, You shall love as yourself those near you. There is no other commandment greater than these. 32. And the scribe said, Honestly, Teacher, you have truthfully said that He is One. There is none other: 33. and to love Him with all the heart, and with the bringing together of your understanding, and with all your ability and strength, and to love a neighbor as yourself, is more than all whole burnt offerings and sacrifices. 34. And when Jesus saw that he answered wisely, He said, You are not far from the kingdom of God. After that no man had the courage to ask any questions. 35. And Jesus continued teaching in the temple, How can the scribes say that Christ is the Son of David? 36. For David himself said by the Holy Spirit, The Lord said to my Lord, Sit on my right hand, until I make your enemies your footstool. 37. David himself called Him Lord; then how can He also be David's son? And the great mass of people heard Him gladly. (Mark 12:28-37 EDNT)

The essential elements of faith-based behavior are in the Beatitudes (Matthew 5:3-11). Those who live the new faith-based behavior must have a sense of spiritual neediness, be sorry for their sinful ways, become humble-minded, and seek moral justice for the less fortunate. They willingly show compassion toward others with a clean heart and become peacemakers who suffer persecution gracefully with no mixed motives.

The discipline of the Christian lifestyle is a system of guidelines affecting passion and behavior; **passion** is the powerful or compelling emotion and feeling one has about life and living, while **behavior** deals with actions, deeds, manners, guided by life-goals. The rules imply instruction and correction that improves, molds, strengthens, and perfects character and goal directed activity. The Way of Jesus produces a moral education that guides decent and moral discipline that corrects and improves lifestyle performance and accomplishments. The change of heart that comes with salvation provides a new acceptance of spiritual authority and a new perspective on life itself. This prepares one for a new lifestyle and a moral purpose for living. It also opens spiritual eyes so a new believer can see a way forward in spite of the troubled seas. The words of M. J. Cartwright (1889) to the Old Ship of Zion describes this part of the journey and speaks to the decision to board the ship for the great adventure known as the Christian way of life.

I was drifting away on life's pitiless sea,
And the angry waves threatened my ruin to be,
When away at my side, there I dimly descried,
A stately old vessel, and loudly I cried:
"Ship ahoy! Ship ahoy!"
And loudly I cried: "Ship ahoy!"

'Twas the "old ship of Zion," thus sailing along,
All aboard her seemed joyous, I heard their sweet song;
And the Captain's kind ear, ever ready to hear,
Caught my wail of distress, as I cried out in fear:
"Ship ahoy! Ship ahoy!"
As I cried out in fear: "Ship ahoy!"

The good Captain commanded a boat to be low'red,
And with tender compassion He took me on board;
And I'm happy today, all my sins washed away
In the blood of my Savior, and now I can say:
"Bless the Lord! Bless the Lord!"

From my soul I can say: "Bless the Lord!"

O soul, sinking down 'neath sin's merciless wave,
The strong arm of our Captain is mighty to save;
Then trust Him today, no longer delay,
Board the old ship of Zion, and shout on your way:
"Jesus saves! Jesus saves!"
Shout and sing on your way: "Jesus saves!"

— M. J. Cartwright (1889)

Zion is used as a synonym for Jerusalem and was first used in
II Samuel 5:7.

The Gospel Lighthouse

Faith-based behavior produces spiritual influence. Those who live the faith-based life of the Beatitudes will enjoy the threefold principle of influence: **salt, light**, and a **city** built on a hill.

Salt: preserves and prevents corruption, a salted faith-based behavior preserves a healthy lifestyle and prevents dishonesty. (Luke 14:34)

Light: points the way and guides the steps, enlightened behavior brings brightness to the day and illuminates the darkness of the night. (Matthew 5:16; 1 John 1:7)

City: the walled cities of Bible days were places of safety and faith-based behavior that became a shining city on a hill that, a lighthouse or a guiding beacon to the troubled and weary traveler. (Matthew 5:14, 16)

The Beatitudes come from the opening verses of the Sermon on the Mount delivered by Jesus. (Matthew 5:3-12). Each one tells something about an attitude or a predisposition to act that one should have as a believer. The key to the blessings in these statements by Jesus is action. It is not only being, but also doing that causes a believer to become a bright and shinning light to the world. This light will cause others to observe the individual's moral behavior and glorify God. Seeing the light of a believer's personal behavior can bring peace to a troubled soul. This is true faith-based influence. The words of the song, The Lighthouse show that believers can become a guiding light to those struggling in troubled waters. The local places of worship and the meeting of faith-based groups become a beacon shining as a lighthouse to all who sail on life's rough seas.

There's a lighthouse on the hillside
That overlooks the sea
When I'm tossed it sends out a light
That I might see
And the light that shines in darkness now
Will safely lead me o'er
If it wasn't for the lighthouse
My ship would be no more.

(Narrative)
It seems that everybody about us says,
Tear that old lighthouse down
The big ships just don't pass this way anymore.
So there›s no use in standing around
Then my mind goes back to that one dark, stormy night
When just in time, I saw the light.

Yes, it was the light form that old lighthouse
That stands up there on the hill.

— Hinson

Rescue the Perishing

Many of the early gospel songs had a missionary and seafaring theme because believers of that day were familiar with sailing ships and the hazards of the sea. Frances (Fanny) J. Crosby (1820-1915) wrote the lyrics to many Christian hymns. She was blind resulting from malpractice of a doctor when she was six weeks old. When her mother realized that Fanny would be shut out from all the beauties of the natural world, she told Fanny that two of the world's greatest poets, Homer and Milton, were blind and at times God deprived some of physical ability in order to develop their spiritual insight. Fanny's father died when she was just seven months old leaving her mother a widow at age 21. While her mother worked as a domestic servant for others, Fanny's grandmother educated her and became her eyes. The grandmother described the world of colors, sunsets and sunrises, rainbows and the beauty of nature to Fanny so well that Fanny could "see" the colors in her mind. She wrote as a young girl "Soon I learned what other children possessed, but I made up my mind to store away a little jewel in my heart, which I called Content." That content was the substance and source for the lyrics of her songs.

Believers have sung Fanny's songs for many years. Hymns such as Blessed Assurance; Safe in the Arms of Jesus, and Rescue the Perishing. Her lyrics brought comfort, witness, and she often used seafaring themes, one being Rescue the Perishing (1869):

> Rescue the perishing, care for the dying,
> Snatch them in pity from sin and the grave;
> Weep o'er the erring one, lift up the fallen,
> Tell them of Jesus, the mighty to save.
> Rescue the perishing, care for the dying,
> Jesus is merciful, Jesus will save.

Two events in the winter of 1850, when Fanny was 30 years old, further shaped her life. When Fanny realized that she had followed her mother and grandmother's religion, but had not made a personal choice, she made a decision to accept Christ. The other event was an epidemic of cholera in which she willingly assisted the sick. During this period Fanny wrote, "The Lord planted a star in my life and no cloud has ever obscured its light." Believers of today have little excuse for failing to have a lifestyle of witness when comparing their limitations vs. accomplishments with those of Fanny Crosby and others.

First Steps of Faith

The idea of being called "Christian" was used first by the public (Acts 11:26) when they recognized the way the converts at Antioch behaved and the changes in their daily lifestyle. They called them "Messiah-like" because of their lifestyle. Later, the word became an identity for those who followed Christ. Some dislike the use of the word, because it no longer means who you are, but defines your membership or place of worship. The word "Christian" is a misnomer because the true process is not followed: first one becomes a convert (believer), next they become a disciple (learner), as disciples mature they are trusted and sent with a message (apostle), then comes a lifestyle of witness that brings glory to Christ. [At times in this book, I use the word "believer" instead of the general term "Christian" to be more specific.]

Transact Their Affairs as Christians

19. They that were distributed in foreign lands because of the persecution of Stephen went as far as Phoenicia, speaking of Christ only to the Jews. 20. But some were natives of Cyprus and Cyrene, on their arrival at Antioch, they began to speak to the Greeks also, announcing the Lord Jesus. 21. And the power of the Lord was with them and a great number believed and turned to the Lord. 22. And when the news was reported to the assembly in Jerusalem: they sent Barnabas to Antioch. 23. When he arrived and saw the grace of God he was glad and continuously encouraged them to remain with the Lord with readiness of heart. 24. For he was a good man and full of the Holy Spirit and faith: and many people were added to the Lord. 25. Then Barnabas went to Tarsus in search of Saul: 26. and when he found Saul brought him to Antioch. And for one whole year they assembled with the church and taught many people. And the disciples first began to transact their affairs as Christians in Antioch. (Acts 11:19-26 EDNT) [At first it was a life-style recognized by others, then it became a mark of identification as a follower of Christ.]

Lifestyle first recognized by society when believers began to transact business in a different manner. All believers are in full-time Christian service. Confession of sin, conversion and regeneration are sufficient foundation for lifestyle witness. Water Baptism is sufficient identification with God, the Father, Jesus, the Son, and the Holy Spirit to proclaim public acknowledgement and credentials for full-time Kingdom service for the believer.

The watered-down message of religious leaders has changed the term "Christian" to meet the lower personal standards of various sectarian groups. In many circles, the word "Christian" does not presently mean a true believer in Jesus Christ, one who has confessed personal sins, professed redemption confirmed by a changed lifestyle where one becomes a witness by a changed life. It has become a simple identification for those who occasionally attend a church service regardless of their lifestyle during the week. This is contrary to the image of a believer presented in sacred writings and sends a weak message to the unconverted in the community. The watered-down message creates weak links in the chain of evangelism and provides an image of wimpy leadership with weak, timid, unassertive or ineffectual followers.

WIMP – Weak Interacting Ministry Partners

When outsiders see weak leadership and feeble followers, they naturally assume that all of Christianity has **W**eak **I**nteracting **M**inistry **P**artners. When there is a feeble effort to work and witness together to reach the community with the message of personal salvation, a puny response will follow. When ministry workers fail to become partners with community leaders to meet the needs of the people, their lack of compassion and concern cannot be justified. Such weak links in the outreach chain limit the advance of the Gospel. Jesus was clear in His disappointment of those who neglected even "the least" opportunity to serve the needs of the disadvantaged.

Commitment to Win

13. For it is God working in you to make you both willing and able to do His good pleasure. 14. Do all things without grumbling and disagreements: 15. that you may be above suspicion and unblemished, the children of God, with an untarnished reputation, in the midst of a warped and twisted nation, where you shine as lights in the world; 16. holding forth the word of life; that you give me grounds for rejoicing on the day of Christ, that my course was run successfully, and my labor was fruitful. 17. Yes, and even if my blood must be poured out as a sacrifice to nurture your faith, I shall rejoice and share your joy. 18. And in the same manner you joy and share my rejoicing. (Philippians 2:13-18 EDNT

An Olympic Spirit

The mystical and global spirit that brings young athletes together with inspiriting and ageing sports enthusiasts from 200 countries to a single venue remains a mystery. Every four years somewhere in the world, these aspiring athletes gather to compete for gold, silver, or bronze medals. Only one in each category will win the gold, but they all sacrifice their time to training and deny themselves much of their social life just to spend hours each day of grueling training. Overcoming financial and physical limitations, they spend years pursuing a fleeting prize. Why can't this "spirit" be part of the development of young Christians?

Paul's Olympic-type Experience

22. I am made all things to all men that I might by all means save some. 23. I am still doing this to advance the gospel, so that I may become a joint-partaker of the gospel with you. 24. Do you not know that they who run in a race all run, but only one receives the prize? So run that you may obtain the prize. 25. And every man who enters the race practices rigid self-control. They do this to win a wreath that will soon wither, but we seek a crown that will not fade. 26. I run but not aimlessly; so I fight, but not as a shadow boxer: 27. but I beat my body black and

blue, and bring it into subjection: lest by any means, when I have preached to others, I myself should be rejected as a worthless coin. (I Corinthians 9:22-27 EDNT)

Appropriate Godly Behavior

17. Give all men their due; to the band of believers your habitual love; to God, your worship; to the leader owed respect. 18. Respect the authority of those you serve, line up under the authority not only to those who are kind and considerate, but also to those who are hard to please. 19. It is a sign of grace when one bears up under unjust suffering because of moral goodness in his heart. 20. When you do wrong, do you suffer quietly a blow from the hand? But if you do things right and still suffer calmly, this is appropriate godly behavior. (1 Peter 2:17-20 EDNT)

Should one compare the Olympic Spirit with the weak witness of many faith-based groups, there can be no justification for their lack of performance. Where are the role models? Where are the heroes of faith? A simple question is asked of faith-based leaders, "What happened to the "go ye" in the heart of early believers and the spirit of martyrdom that propelled pristine believers into an unfriendly world to establish a moral lifestyle?"

Run the Course

1. Therefore, since we are watched from above by such a cloud of witnesses, let us rid ourselves of all that weighs us down, and the sin that so persistently surrounds us, and **let us run with steadfast endurance, the course that is marked out before us**, 2. let this fix your eyes on Jesus the origin and the crown of all faith, who, to win His prize of blessedness, endured the cross and made light of its shame, Jesus, who now sits on the right of God's throne. 3. Consider Him who steadfastly endured such opposition at the hands of sinners, and **compare your lives with His, so that you may not faint and grow weary in your souls**. 4. you have not yet had to resist to the point of blood in your struggle against sin. (Hebrews 12:1-6 EDNT)

In the Gospels, God comes closer to the creation through the Incarnation (John 1:14). This produced a more intimate basis for fellowship with the human race. Jesus came to dwell on earth and experience the hardship and difficulties, the same ones we all face every day. The participation of Jesus in earthly affairs and His willingness to share the plight of the human family clearly bear witness of God's desire for communion and fellowship with the human race. Calvary provided a new dimension to this fellowship by opening access to salvation to the whole world.

The conversation between God and the human family was broken when sin entered the Garden. Dialogue after this great separation was painful. When Adam and Eve heard the voice of God in the Garden, they hid themselves from the presence of God among the trees of the Garden. When God spoke Adam answered, "I heard your voice in the garden, and I was afraid." (Genesis 3:7-24) Many today attempt to avoid the searching experience of spiritual conviction even though it is the path to re-establish a mutually and enjoyable conversation with God. Calvary brought reconciliation between God and the human race. All converts to the Christian faith will experience lifestyle challenges. God's program to deal with these difficulties includes confession, conversion, communion, and the collect in worship.

Confession is both a declaration of guilt and an affirmation of faith that brings forgiveness from God. When one personally acknowledges sinful acts and seeks forgiveness, the confession of God's grace becomes active. A true confession of sinfulness becomes a profession of faith in a Savior. Such a declaration brings about a conversion. This produces an exchanged life: the old ways for a new and living way of life. The transfer of guilt and sins to the Christ brings about a change of behavior that produces a moral lifestyle. This change brings into being a overhaul of the old behavior that followed sinful ways and a conversion of both soul and spirit into a living witness for the Christian way of life. Peter wrote of the precious and treasured promises that come with conversion:

> 3. Since His divine power has bestowed upon us all things that are necessary for true life and true worship, through the full knowledge of Him who called us to His own glory and moral uprightness: 4. Since through these gifts He has bestowed upon us precious and treasured promises: you are to share the divine nature, leaving behind the corruption and passions of the world. 5. And you too have to contribute every effort on your own part, crowning your faith with moral excellence, and to moral excellence knowledge from books and teachers: 6. and to your knowledge self-control; and to self-control enduring steadfastness, and to enduring steadfastness godly worship; 7. and to godly worship brotherly kindness; and to brotherly kindness benevolent love.
> (2 Peter 1:3-7 EDNT)

Traveling the Way of Christ is a lifestyle of behavior that honors God, Nation, family, and personal values. Those who have experience confession and conversion enjoy the precious and treasured promises of God. Salvation is available to anyone willing to board the Old Gospel Ship.

> 13. By this we know that we remain in Him and He in us, because He has given us of the Spirit. 14. And we have beheld and bear witness that the Father has sent the Son as Savior of the world. 15. **Whoever confesses that Jesus is the Son of God, God remains in him and he remains in God. 16. And we have known and have believed the love which God has given to us. God is love; and the ones remaining in love remain in God and God in him remains.** 17. Herein is our love made complete, that we may have confidence in the Day of Judgment, because as that One is, so are we in the world. (1 John 4: 13-17 EDNT)

Confession and conversion are similar or almost synonymous. Both share sameness and seem to be cut out of the same cloth. Each requires the other to complete a process. A confession of sin and a profession of faith produce a conversion that leads to changes in behavior. Conversion transforms actions, deeds, manners and establishes a moral lifestyle and straightforward behavior. With the admission of sinful ways, God will guide the penitent to a walk of the Calvary road and this repenting soul will experience conversion. The contrite spirit moves the Heart of God in forgiveness for the confessor and brings personal joy in conversion and rejoicing in the presence of the Angels in heaven. (Luke 15:7, 10) The rejoicing in heaven is by Jesus Himself, because the Angels do not fully understand the forgiveness of sins. Although confession of sins is the defining moment in conversion, God, the Father, is the forgiver of sins. When an individual turns from sinful ways to God for forgiveness, it is Jesus, the Son of God, who assures the believer of salvation. Jesus, because of the sacrifice of Calvary, is the Mediator between God and the penitent. It is Jesus, who mediates the difference between God and the human race. Jesus is not a neutral mediator; He is personally involved in the process. The primary work of Jesus was to save sinners. An extreme example of God's longsuffering is the conversion of Saul of Tarsus who became the great Apostle Paul:

> 12. Thanks I give to the One empowering me, Christ Jesus our Lord, because He deemed me faithful putting me in His service, 13. Who was a blasphemer, a persecutor, a man of violence, author of outrage, and yet He had mercy on me, because I was acting in the ignorance of unbelief. 14. But the grace of our Lord was more than abundant with faith and love which is in Christ Jesus. 15. **What a true saying and worthy of a favorable reception, that Christ Jesus came to the world to save sinners;** of whom I rank first. 16. And yet I was pardoned, so that in me first Christ Jesus might give an **extreme example of His longsuffering**; I was to be a precedent for all those who will ever believe in Him and win eternal life.
> (1 Timothy 1:12-16 EDNT)

Taking the faith step toward God brings transformation and an enjoyable relationship with both God and other believers. Conversion comes when one walks the Calvary road and experiences the transformation of both internal life changes and external lifestyle behavior. An awareness of personal sinfulness is required to produce a redirection toward God in absolute surrender to His will. The Calvary encounter begins in confession and conversion and continues in communion. At conversion, an individual accepts forgiveness of sins and gains fellowship with God, and begins the lifelong journey toward heaven. With communion, the process is continued and corrected to guarantee continued fellowship with God.

Communion should be preceded by confession designed to keep the personal experience of believers relevant and worthy of God's blessings. Communion is a commemoration to remember the Last Supper of Jesus with His disciples before His Crucifixion. The elements of consecrated bread and wine represent an intimacy with Christ and a spiritual closeness with other believers. It is an emotional connection with a sense of shared spiritual identity and fellowship with other believers. Unlike water baptism, a onetime event, Communion is a practice repeated throughout the life of a believer. It is a time of worship when believers corporately come together as one body to remember and celebrate what Christ achieved on Calvary. Believers observe Communion because Jesus told His followers to remember His death in this manner. It is a time to remember the life, death and resurrection of Jesus. Those who observe communion must examine their life less they become unworthy participants.

> 27. And in conclusion, whoever shall eat this bread and drink this cup of the Lord, in **an unworthy manner**, shall be guilty of violating the body and blood of the Lord. 28. Each time let a man examine himself before he eats of that bread and drinks of that cup. 29. **The reason for self-examination before eating and drinking is to prevent partaking in an unworthy manner when one does not properly consider the Lord's assembly.** 30. For this reason many are powerless and sick among you and

many die. 31. For if we judge ourselves rightly, we should not be judged by God. 32. But when we are judged, we are disciplined of the Lord that we should not be condemned eternally with the world. 33. Wherefore, my brethren, when you come together to eat, wait in turn for a proper distribution. (1 Corinthians 11:27-33 EDNT)

Collect in Christian worship is both an act of worship and a short general prayer as a dialog between the minister and the people. In the Middle Ages, the prayer was referred to in Latin as collectio, but in some churches it follows a hymn of praise early in the service. (Tragically, some present day churches miss the point of the collectio, and use this prayer time to take a collection or offering.) A true collect starts with the minister's greeting, "The Lord be with you", to which the people respond, "And also with you." The minister then invites all to pray by saying, "Let us pray." In ancient practice, an invitation to kneel was given and the people spent a short time in silent prayer, after which they were invited to stand. Then, the minister concluded the time of prayer by **"collecting"** their prayers in a unified petition, referred to as a **collect**. Two examples of Collects from the (1662) English Book of Common Prayer:

[1] Almighty God, to whom all hearts be open, all desires known, and from whom no secrets are hid; Cleanse the thoughts of our hearts by the inspiration of thy Holy Spirit, that we may perfectly love thee, and worthily magnify thy holy Name; through Christ our Lord. Amen.

[2] O God, the King eternal, whose light divides the day from the night and turns the shadow of death into the morning: drive far from us all wrong desires, incline our hearts to keep your law, and guide our feet into the way of peace; that, having done your will with cheerfulness during the day, we may, when night comes, rejoice to give you thanks; through Jesus Christ our Lord. Amen.

The spirit of prayer is more precious than treasure of gold and silver. Pray often, for prayer is a shield to the soul, a sacrifice to God, and a scourge for Satan.

— John Bunyan

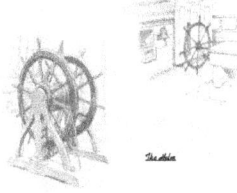

CHAPTER THREE

Navigating Contrary Winds

…. through the narrow gorge in the shadow of the grave and fear no evil. God is my authority and provides a skilled crew to comfort me. (Psalms 23:4 DOT)

9. For this purpose, since the day we heard it, we have not ceased to pray for you and to desire that you might be filled with the knowledge of His will in all wisdom and spiritual understanding; 10. that you might **behave worthy of the pleasing of the Lord**, personally bearing good fruit and increasing in the full knowledge of God; 11. being empowered according to His glorious power, with a cheerful exercise of endurance and unlimited perseverance; 12. joyously giving thanks to the Father, who made us sufficient to partake of the inheritance of the saints who live in the light: 13. who has rescued us from the dominion of darkness, and has transformed us into the kingdom of His dear Son: 14. in whom we have redemption through His blood, even the forgiveness of sins: (Colossians 1:9-14 EDNT).

It is the Set of the Sails

The early excitement following conversion often fades as one engages the daily challenges of life. Just as believers rely on the power of the Spirit to stay on course, a sailing ship depends on available wind power to move forward. When the ship encounters contrary winds, the crew uses special tactics to navigate through the opposing weather and continue to move forward on the charter course. Contrary winds require a change in the placement of the sails to take full advantage of the blustery weather. It was not the direction of the wind, but the set of the sails that controlled the course of the ship. The ship had a primary course established at the beginning of the journey; the ship's crew must now adjust the sail to avail the ship of the available wind. This is called tacking; a course of action intended to change the orientation of the sails to assure a forward direction. Seafaring means following the sea as a trade, business, or calling. While "seafaring" was still clear in the minds of most, Ella Wilcox wrote these lyrics 'Tis the Set of the Sail:

> One ship sails East,
> And another West,
> By the self-same winds that blow,
> 'Tis the set of the sails
> And not the gales,
> That tells the way we go.
> Like the winds of the sea
> Are the waves of time,
> As we journey along through life,
> 'Tis the set of the soul,
> That determines the goal,
> And not the calm or the strife.

— Ella Wheeler Wilcox (1916)

Forward in spite of Difficulties

Everyone has difficulties; life is not easy. This story reveals that in the midst of difficult times, God can enable a believer to be productive as a witness. In spite of the contrary winds of family illness and persecution, John Bunyan became a popular writer. These facts show how God works wonders to advance the Gospel. It seems that King Charles II of England in 1660 was trying to reestablish the power of the Church of

England. The King ordered the closure of all non-Anglican churches, making the preaching of the Gospel in any place other than an established church an act of treason. John Bunyan refusing to curtail his ministry continued holding a worship service in a friend's home. At this, a local constable arrested him and imprisoned for the next twelve years. During this period, his family suffered and his blind daughter died, but Bunyan was undaunted. He supported his family in prison by making lace; but in his solitude discovered a gift of writing. His fame as an imprisoned writer increased the sale of his writings and he eventually wrote sixty books. His most famous book, The Pilgrim's Progress, was a best seller during his lifetime and sold millions since his death. This book became the most popular book in English except the Bible. Bunyan continued to write and minister in spite of bad health. His deathbed ramblings were a dying man speaking to a living church. His wife recorded some of his sayings and published as *Mr. Bunyan's Dying Sayings*. One such statement speaks to the value of prayer:

> "The spirit of prayer is more precious than treasure of gold and silver. Pray often, for prayer is a shield to the soul, a sacrifice to God, and a scourge for Satan."

Monuments and Memorials

Believers around the world encounter various forms of conflict and opposition: from mere resentment to public persecution. Yet, history demonstrates that God brings deliverance from all kinds of difficulties. The changing winds of politics, revolutions, social conflicts, and wars make significant changes in cultures, societies and nations. During momentous social changes, it becomes difficult for believers to remain steadfastly committed to scriptural authority for influence and lifestyle guidance. Throughout history, **monuments** were to remember significant human events and **memorials** take into account noteworthy people. This has become a tradition, almost without knowing, that Christianity observes. Church buildings have become monuments to architects and donors rather than places of worship.

When a society such as the USSR deteriorates into a godless culture, the traditional houses of worship become Russian monuments to the politics of the times. It became evident that as a culture moves toward a godless society, the people neglect the sacraments; such as, baptism, communion, matrimony, and holy orders. They discontinue or relegate the sacred to routine or civil events without spiritual significance. During the days of the USSR, the neglect of Christian sacraments by the people and totally absent from the political leadership; however, the last Foreign Minister, Shevardnadze, following resignation at the collapse of the USSR in 1991 immediately submitted to water baptism in the Georgian Orthodox Church.

A monument is a public expression of a single powerful idea in a single emphatic form, on a colossal scale and in permanent materials, made to serve the public. A monument because they are public must be clearly readable. Monuments incorporate a few ancient types: the triumphal arch, the colossal column, the sanctuary, the mural shrine, the Wailing Wall, and other timeless forms. Most church buildings are foursquare citadels with an architectural point-marker pointing to the sky. Each Architect provides a secular interpretation to mark a particular sectarian distinctive rather than creating a "mission station" to reach the lost. The monuments may become a "hospital for wounded souls," but not a triumphant witness to the redemptive work of Christ. This is a departure from the New Testament, where "from house to house" believers ceased not to teach and preach Jesus Christ, where the Christian witness was a lifestyle that brought evangelism to the community and to the marketplace.

Peter's Significant Sermon

> 38. ... Everyone must repent for the forgiveness of sins
> and be baptized in the Name of Jesus Christ, and also

you shall receive the gift of the Holy Spirit. 39. Because the promise is to you, and your children, and to all those in distant places, even as many as the Lord, our God shall call. 40. And with many other words did he testify and exhort, saying, Rescue yourselves from this troublesome generation. 41. Those who willingly received his word, were baptized: and the same day about three thousand souls were added to the believers. 42. **And they continued consistently in the apostles' doctrine and fellowship, and in breaking of bread, and in prayers.** (Acts 2:38-42 EDNT)

42. **And every day in the temple and in every house, they ceased not to teach and preach Jesus Christ.** (Acts 5:42 EDNT)

Paul's Message to Asian Believers

20. And you know I delivered the message to you and kept back nothing that was good for you, **having taught you publicly and from house to house.** 21. Witnessing to the Jews and to the Greeks about the necessity of repentance before God and faith toward our Lord Jesus Christ. (Acts 20: 20-21 EDNT)

A memorial is a witness to a deep human need expressed by understood symbols that bring resolution and closure. A marker at a roadside accident noting the death of a friend becomes a memorial. A refreshing of such memorials must be continuous or they soon fade and the travelers fail to remember the significance of the effort. Christian communion is a sacred memorial observing the death of Jesus using the understood symbols of bread and wine. Wine representing the shed blood of Christ and broken bread as a symbol of the body of Jesus sacrificially broken.

Paul reminding that Jesus Instituted Communion

17. In giving this charge I mention a practice that I cannot commend, **you gather for worship not for good, but for the worse.** 18. In the first place, when you come together, I hear there are divisions among you and I have reason to believe it. 19. There must be dissent and factions among

you, so those approved may become obvious among you. 20. **You come together socially to eat, but it is not the Lord's Supper.** 21. For some being hungry eat hurriedly before the poor and some are frequently drunk. 22. You do have houses to eat and drink in, don't you? Or do you look down on the poor and embarrass the church? What shall I say about this? **Certainly, I will not praise you for this behavior.** 23. For I have received an understanding from the Lord of that which I deliver to you, that the Lord Jesus the same night in which He was being betrayed took bread: 24. After He gave thanks, He broke it, saying to the disciples, this represents My body given for you: this do often to recall to memory my sacrifice. 25. In the same manner when supper was ended he took the cup, saying, this cup represents the New Testament ratified by my blood: every time you do this recall to memory my sacrifice. **26. As often as you repeat this, eat the bead and drink the cup, you proclaim the Lord's death until He returns.** (1 Corinthians 11:17-26 EDNT)

The Power to Move Forward

In the Scripture, wind, fire, and oil were symbols of the Holy Spirit. Spiritual wind is the power that moves a believer forward on the charted direction. There was a mighty wind at the close of the Jewish Harvest Festival. When the believers assembled in harmony in one place, there was sound carried by a violent wind from the heavens, and those gathered together were precipitants of an infilling of the Holy Spirit. The Spirit both empowered them and made possible the forward march of the Gospel. There would be opposition and persecution, but the Spirit became their divine guide to keep them on course. The Spirit was a companion walking along side to protect and defend against all that would carry them off course. When contrary winds produce waves of opposition, believers must follow the instructions to keep the Old Gospel Ship sailing in the direction of heaven. Isaiah reminded Israel to follow seafaring rules to stay on course.

When adversity comes remember your instructions and recall the information and you will understand from the past the course you must sail. You will know the choice to make. (Isaiah 30.20, 21 DOT)

Contrary Winds

There is no way to avoid the contrary winds, the ship and crew must use the force of the wind to move in a forward direction and stay on course. When the helmsman steering the ship faces contrary winds, he will call to the crew "Ready About." This signals the crew to ready the lines that control the sails. The crew must make sure the lines are not tangled and are free of any obstruction that would hinder carrying out the helmsman's orders.

When the crew has readied the lines, the crew will yell, *"Ready."*

The helmsman will then command, *"Hard Alee"* to notify the crew to initiate the turn through the wind. It is important that the ship have enough momentum to carry itself through the turn. As the boat makes the turn, the bow of the sailing ship begins to point more directly into the wind and the sails will begin to flutter. It is a common mistake for novice sailors to over tighten the lines before the ship changes directions and the boat increases speed and turns more into the wind. The crew has rules for both weak and strong winds.

Once the sailing ship has finished turning and the sails begin to fill, the trimming of the sails assure the right direction. These maneuvers are not easy and are usually learned through experience. Repeated trial and error teaches these lessons. When conditions call for "all hands on deck," with each crew member handling the lines, they learn the ropes to set the sails for contrary winds.

Establishing Priorities

12. Not as though I had already won the battle or were already faultless: but I pursue, if I may catch that for which also I was captured by Christ Jesus. 13. Brothers, I have not yet reached my goal: **but this one thing I do,** forgetting those things that are behind, and stretching forth to those

things that are before, 14. I press on to secure the goal and the prize of the high calling of God in Christ Jesus. 15. Let us therefore, as many as are mature, be thus minded: and if in anything you be otherwise minded, God will reveal this to you. 16. **Nevertheless, we must continue to live up to what we have attained, and behave the same rule, and mind the same thing.** (Philippians 3:12-16 EDNT)

Negative Behavior that Destroys

Human beings have a tendency to develop negative behavior that wipes out the possibility of future achievements. Many seem bent on self-destruction while others attempt to take down as many as possible to the lowest common denominator of life. At their lowest level, there are no steps upward, no ladder to the top, not a rope of hope and seemingly no redemption. Worse than any of the animal kingdom, the human race engages in behavior that ultimately destroys. They lie, cheat and steal, in the process of negative behavior that is hurtful to everyone around them. Lies often show deep psychological needs; such as, a lack of self-esteem or self-image. The fact that people cheat on their mates as well as their taxes, shows the scope and acceptance of negative behavior. In addition, some may steal because of personal or family needs, but even rich people steal. Those who suffer from kleptomania steal just for the thrill and the adrenalin rush. When individuals cling to bad habits; such as, gambling, gossiping and bullying, they become sources of stress. This robs productivity and personal peace and greatly hinders moral leadership.

Dealing with Temptations

All faith-based people are tempted no matter how closely they following the course charted by their faith. Satan entices and lures with excitement; temptation is the desire for something that is wrong that one will regret later. Believers must grow stronger and smarter to win the battle against wrong behavior. There are steps a believer may take to avoid yielding to temptation. When individuals served

Satan, they are pushed toward things that are evil; however, a convert to Christianity has the enabling of the Holy Spirit to assist their choice when temptation comes. James wrote temptation and saw it as a choice, "Rejoice because you have a choice."(James 1:2) When one stands at the forks of the road with one leading down and the other rising upward, they should rejoice because they have a choice. Making the right choice is the way to overcome wrong behavior. It takes a lifetime to gain full strength to avoid yielding to temptations. Follow these three steps:

Step one: Do not be caught off guard or surprised by temptation. Control the tendency to yield to bad behavior. To recognize one's human weakness is the first step to be prepared for temptation. James 1:12 explains that individuals are tempted when they are enticed by natural desires. Paul explains in 1 Corinthians 10:13 that the temptations of one is no different from what others experience. Paul shared that God will make a way of escape for the tempted if they will only follow His guidance. With each temptation, the believer should look for the way out that God provides and take it quickly.

Step two: Control your sensual desires was exemplified in the Old Testament by Joseph when he refused the sexual advances from the wife of his boss. (Genesis 39:10) The New Testament is filled with references explaining the best way to resist temptation is to walk away (1 Corinthians 6:18; 1 Corinthians 10:14; 1 Timothy 6:11; 2 Timothy 2:22).

Step three: Use the weapon of the Word to resist temptation.

Read (2 Corinthians 10:4 – 5) to understand how to use the Word, one of the spiritual weapons. At the first sight of temptation, it would not be practical to read the Bible, but you can "hide the word in your heart" and it will keep you for sin. When one is overtaken in a fault or makes a misstep, they must repent quickly, because believers must not continue to practice or indulge in wrong behavior (Galatians 6:1).

Practical counsel from and prayer with other believers is a good weapon against future temptation. Prayer is a weapon against falling into sin because of temptation, remember the spiritual soul is willing but the human body is weak (Matthew 26:41); therefore, believers must be on guard.

Bad things Happen to Good People

Three kinds of difficulties bring anguish and distress to the life of believers. Appreciating the value of God; that is, seeing the worth of God in your life brings strength and encouragement to those who experience difficult times. (1) God chastens or disciplines those He loves. This is a good thing! (2) Trials, suffering, and persecutions come to test the fiber of faith. When one passes through and adequately completes a period of testing, they are stronger to withstand Satan's snares. (3) Temptations or tricks from Satan may ensnare, but nothing happens to believers that they cannot handle with enablement of the Holy Spirit and the fellowship support from other believers. How does one avoid these difficulties? Pray this simple prayer: **God help me to remember that nothing will happen to me today that you and I together can't handle.**

Believers must not be spiritual wimps. God may test believers, but God does not tempt individuals beyond their ability to resist sin. God built a hedge around His servant Job and permitted Satan to test Job sorely, but in all his trouble, Job did not sin against God. (Job 2:4-10) Paul wrote to the Corinthians believers about Satan's schemes and that they should be careful not to permit Satan to outsmart them. (2 Corinthians 2:11) Pride opens the path to destruction and an arrogant spirit is present before a fall (Proverbs 16:18). Most difficulties can be overcome by handling problems in the light of day and resist giving the devil a foothold (Ephesians 4:26b - 27).

The Enticement of Testing

12. Blood related and fortunate is the man who flinches not under the enticement of testing: for when he is proved trustworthy, he shall be given the wreath of honor that verifies vitality, which God promised to all who worship out of a benevolent heart. 13. Let no man say when he is enticed, God allured me to evil: for God does not use wickedness to validate the trustworthiness of any man. 14. But every man is attracted to wicked deeds, when he chooses action based on personal desire, and hope of pleasure. 15. Then when personal desire has joined together with enticement, it produces a voluntary transgression: and this offense produces separation from observant morality, and at the end separation from God. (James 1:12-15 EDNT)

Oswald J. Chambers, a prominent early twentieth century Scottish minister and writer is known for his book, My Utmost for His Highest. In his devotional Chambers wrote "A man's disposition on the inside, i.e., what he possesses in his personality, determines what he is tempted by on the outside." (1 John 5:18; James 1:13-14; Hebrews 2:18)

Believers are not Alone

Believers live among and are supported by a fellowship that is a band of believers. Spiritual fellowship and the moral example of others bring strength and encouragement to believers. Satan is the enemy of those who journey with Christ and is always seeking ways and means to discourage or disgrace those who follow Jesus. Believers must exercise self-control, always be vigilant, and stand firm in their faith. There is spiritual guidance from other believers and scriptural assistance for those tempted. (Romans 6:11-13; 2 Timothy 4:18; Ephesians 6:10, 13; Galatians 5:16 – 17; 1 Peter 5:8-10; 1 John 5:18) Prior to conversion, evil forces pushed individuals into bad situations and made it easy to go the wrong way;

however, conversion brought a regeneration of the mind, will, and the emotions and now believers have a choice in times of temptation. They can now rejoice because they have strength to make the right choice.

Rejoice because you have a Choice.

1. James subject to and serving God and the Lord Jesus Christ, to the twelve tribes which are scattered abroad, a cheerful personal greeting. 2. My cherished band of brothers, **count it a jewel (precious stone) when you fall into adversity and testing that gives a choice of direction.** 3. Knowing that your painful trial brings you assurance, trust and works patience. 4. But let suffering have her complete labor and make something of you, that you may be complete in all respects, without defect or omission and whole undivided, and unbroken. 5. If any of you lack wise judgment, let him express the craving by words to God, that gives to all men liberally, and does not defame, chide or snatch away your joy, and it shall be given him. 6. But let him ask in faith, nothing wavering, for he that shows doubt or indecision is like a wave of the sea driven with the wind and tossed. 7. Let not that man think that he shall receive anything of the Lord. 8. A two-spirited man is unsettled and wavering in all his direction, position or manner. (James 1:1-9 EDNT)

The Best Way

The best way to navigate through contrary winds is to follow the instructions set down by those who experienced similar difficulties. Those who traveled the troubled sea of life before have left rules and guiding principles that establish a stable course of action in times of trouble. If one follows the behavior guidelines recommended for troubled waters, they can use the force of contrary winds to move forward and stay on the charted course.

Be Influenced by the Spirit

15. Look carefully how you walk, not foolishly, but in the light, 16. Buying up every opportunity, because these are

evil days. 17. Wherefore be not reckless, but prudently understand the will of the Lord. 18. Stop excessively drinking wine, which influences riotous living; more willingly be influenced by the Spirit; 19. but speak to one another in exalted verse, songs of praise, and sacred music, singing and making melody with the music of your hearts, to the Lord; 20. continue giving thanks to God the Father for all things in the name of our Lord Jesus Christ; 21. line up under one another in reverence to Christ. (Ephesians 5:15-33 EDNT)

Choose life...

CHAPTER FOUR

Behaving the Instructions

I will personally behave cautiously and wisely and I will journey with my family with integrity of heart. (Psalms 101.2)

1. **Become imitators of God, as His beloved children**; 2. and **habitually behave in love**, as Christ loved you, and was delivered for you as an offering and voluntary sacrifice to God to become a pleasing fragrance. 3. But as saints **let not immorality, impurity or callous greediness, be named even once among you; 4. neither obscenity, nor corrupt talking, nor practiced suggestive speech, these are all unbecoming behavior: but rather give thanks**. (Ephesians 5:1-4 EDNT)

A Walk in the Desert

Philip with the Ethiopian Eunuch is a good example of the plan for outreach. Philip was a Deacon in Jerusalem, and the Holy Spirit guided him to take a walk in the desert. There he encountered a searching soul reading the Scroll of Isaiah, but did not understand what he read. Philip joined the man in his chariot, explained the scripture, and led the man to a saving understanding of God's plan. This event clearly demonstrates God's love for the whole world. God prepares the sinner, equips the saint, arranges the situation, supplies the material, and opens the door of opportunity for the searching to find eternal salvation in Jesus. Believers only have to act on the instructions and guidance of the Holy Spirit and the Word. (Acts 8:26-30) Those who hear only have to believe and trust.

The Rabbit and the Turtle

Most everyone has heard the children's story about the race between the rabbit and the turtle. How the rabbit started out fast, but the consistent and steady turtle won the race.   Spiritual growth is slow, progressive and in stages. Normal spiritual development requires a time of becoming. One must learn to believe, learn to obey, learn to trust, learn to follow, and learn to live a moral lifestyle.

Learning to follow Jesus openly and willingly

Part of the lexicon during the seafaring era was the verb "to shanghai." However, there is no "shanghaiing "in Christianity. The concept probably came from the Chinese city of Shanghai, a common destination for the ships with abducted crews. Conscripting or shanghaiing converts just does not work; conversion requires a personal willingness to act in faith. All who board the Ship of Zion must be volunteers and willing to serve the Captain of the Ship and follow the rules that regulate onboard behavior. There are no proselytes in Christianity. All who become Disciples of Christ must personally hear the call with the spiritual ear of the h**ear**t and willingly follow Jesus. There are no "in laws" by marriage in the kingdom of God. God has no grandchildren. Individuals must make a personal decision to follow Christ. It is an individual learning process.

Learning to Believe

It is tragic that the word "be**lie**ve" has a "lie" in the middle. In addition, some folk presently say "believe" when expressing "doubt." For example, in seeking directions some say, "Go to the next crossroad, no I believe it is the second crossroad, then turn right, no I believe from this direction you must turn left." It appears the word "believe" has almost lost spiritual significance in modern culture and language. It has become necessary for one to learn to believe by praying, "Lord, I believe, help my unbelief." Learning to believe may be a rocky road, but the end is worth the journey.

Learning to Obey

Some obey rules out of a fear of punishment; others learn obedience by abiding by the rules and guidance of others. A child often learns to obey by observing the difficulty of others who disobey. Still others learn that it is best to conform to the rules of the house and comply with the instructions of those in charge. Learning to follow the guidance of others is an act of maturity. The first step toward spiritual obedience may be simply to listen to parents and family about the moral road one should walk to become a productive citizen.

Learning to Trust

In order to trust there must be confidence in those with whom you associate. Trust breeds the expectation of hope and this requires one to both desire something and believe it will happen. Without both desire and confidence there will be fear; anxiety that it will not happen or frightened that it will happen. As one grows and understands faith-based behavior, the Christian way of life clearly explained in the ancient scripture, becomes clear. This causes one to become more confident and enables them to trust God and His Word as well as the compelling testimony of others who travel the Right Path.

Learning to Follow

If one desires to walk the path of faith, they should not follow the crowd. The Right Path may be the one less traveled. God warned the ancient Hebrews, when the people of God were longing for a way out of Egypt, they were told "not to follow a multitude to do evil" (Exodus 23:2). The idea of "follow" in scripture suggest chase after or pursue someone or something that is desired. Learning to follow Jesus and maturing believers who walk the Calvary road, requires a sense of urgency. It is crucial that new followers take advantage of every opportunity while favorable conditions exist. Two well-known sayings deal with this important element of growth and development: "Strike while the iron is hot" and "Make hay while the sun shines." Both express urgency to act without hesitation. When one begins the faith journey, they do so because they want a better life and understand it is dangerous to wait until a more favorable day. This should provide an urgency of the moment and supply energy to pursue a moral lifestyle. By closely observing the example of faithful followers of Jesus and taking the same route, one should be able to walk the Right Path with energy and excitement. Walking in fellowship with God and with true believers is an exciting and joyful journey. The eternal reward is worth the long voyage.

Learning to Walk by Faith

The fact that believers must "walk by faith and not by sight" suggests there is a learning process in faith-based behavior. Walking is putting one foot in front of the other at a comfortable distance. When walking, as opposed to running, one foot is always on the ground to provide stability. Spiritual walking is an exercise in faith that in both "the cool of the day and in the heat of the fiery furnace" others are walking with the believer. God walked with Adam and Eve in the "cool of the day." Yet, there was a Fourth Man in the fiery furnace with Shadrach, Meshach, and Abed-nego. These three, known as the Hebrew Children, told Nebuchadnezzar, "Our God whom we serve is able to deliver us from the burning fiery furnace." When the King asked about the condition of the three men who had been bound in their clothes and placed in the over-heated furnace, the servant answered "Did we not cast three men bound...I see four men loose, walking in the midst of the fire" (Daniel 3:13-30).

Perhaps one would have to be there to fully appreciate the miracle of the Hebrew Children. When believers walk in faith remembering the Word, they are as the two disciples on the road to Emmaus declared, "Did not our heart burn within us while He talked with us on the road, and as He explained the scriptures?" (Luke 24:32 EDNT) Walking with believers and understanding the words of Jesus and warm the heart of the coldest individual on planet earth. This is an observable fact of faith-based behavior.

Learning to fly above the Storms

Deep in the writings of Moses, one finds the story of an eagle teaching the young to fly. (Deuteronomy 32:11, 12) The Deuteronomy story goes on to say, "As an eagle would do this with their eaglet, so the Lord with His children." The Children of Israel were accustomed to watching eagles as they soared above their camps. They also observed their nest building in the cliffs and the crags of the highest hillsides. They knew an eagle built a nest out of sticks and stones, sharp things, and then covered it with rabbit fur, down or fern to make a nice, soft bed for their young. The people who followed Moses were also aware of how the eaglets received their flying lessons. A brief review of that process could be instructive for those searching for the Right Path in life.

After the hatching of the eggs, the parents feed the eaglets regularly until they are little butterballs. Every time the eaglets hear the ruffle of a wing, they would close their eyes, open their mouths, and wait for food. The young eaglets would prefer to stay in their soft nest the rest of their lives. It was soft, warm and comfortable with plenty of food and little or no conflict. However, the mother eagle was not satisfied with their failure to face the real world.

Moses described in Deuteronomy how the eagle "stirs up" her nest. After the nest was disturbed, she would flutter above her young. Normally, eaglets would just close their eyes, open their mouth and wait for food, but they were now uncomfortable. Sharp protrusions from the sticks and stones in the nest, was now pricking their tender bodies, so when they heard the fluttering noise they opened their eyes. Then the eagle spread abroad her wings. Can you imagine the thoughts of the young eaglets? "I never saw mother so big before." Could it be that they had never looked. Some would venture up to the side of the nest to avoid the sharp things, others even to the edge of the rocks, but most were fearful of the drastic change coming to their life. Moses described how the mother eagle would take them, put them on her wings, and carry them high into the air.

The young eaglet clutched to its mother's back on its first air ride. It seemed easy, but all of a sudden the mother would jump from beneath the young bird and the eaglet would end up in free fall. Looking up at the majestic wings of their mother and feeling the wind catching the flapping weak wings on their sides, most would get the message, "Hey, I had better do something about this!" Then they would stick out their undeveloped wings in a feeble effort to hold back the wind. They could see the rocks and the trees coming up to meet them. They must have been frightened, but they tried. If the eaglet tried to fly, Job describes how the mother would fold her wings and dart like an arrow beneath the young eaglet, catch the young on her wings, and bear them up again. (Job 9:26; Exodus 19:4) The eaglet probably thought, "I knew mother wouldn't let me down." Then mother would dump the eaglet into the air again, falling, and falling, and falling. The mother repeated this process until the wings were strengthened enough and the young eaglet's courage was strong enough to flap and fly. Remember, the scripture recorded, "As the eagle with the eaglets, so the Lord with His children." This is a lesson we all must learn: we must make an effort before God steps in to assist us.

The other side of this coin is that if the young eaglet did not try to fly, the mother would permit the young bird to fall to the rocks below. God does use conflict and change to create an atmosphere conducive to growth and development, and this creative change can become a place of real achievement or it could destroy you. You decide. Choose life, use your God given wings or your path could lead to destruction.

Lessons from the Eagles

Not only should the young learn from the eaglets about flying, the aging also must learn the special lessons about spiritual health maintenance and continuing to fly above the storm. At times, the old eagles had to learn some hard lessons. The Bible records about the eagle renewing their youth (Psalms 103:5). How do eagles renew their youth? An eagle does not die of old age, they often starve to death. What happens when an eagle ages? A sticky secretion from the nostrils closes off an eagle's sense of smell. When they lose their ability to smell, they lose their taste and consequently their appetite and desire for food.

As aging eagles lose a desire for food, they usually use the last bit of physical strength to fly to some lofty perch so they can watch the rest of the world pass by. They become arrogant and boastful because of memories of hunting, feasting and teaching the young eagles to fly and hunt. Consequently, the old eagle just sits there and starves to death unless some drastic change occurs to transform his attitude. This is where the young eagles assist in the renewal process.

The Role of the Young in Renewal

To assist the renewal of the aging, the young must do some special work. On occasion, some young eagles will sense the difficulty and recognize the problem of an aging eagle. The young eagles will fly past the old one and buzz the roost like a fighter pilot. This attempt to shake the old eagle loose from the lofty perch usually fails. Then the young eagle goes to the valley, kills a warm bloodied animal and takes a piece of the warm, moist flesh and flies back. As they make a close flight past the old eagle with the fresh meat, the young ones eventually get close enough to bump into the old eagle's beak. The juice from the warm meat dissolve a little of the corrosion and the aging eagle senses the taste of food. Hunger begins to rage inside the starving eagle and on the next pass of the young eagle, the old eagle grabs the meat and eats it, and from this gains strength, but the main problem still exists.

Sensing the needs and knowing the answer, the eagle finds a pointed rock. Then the old eagle gets down by the rock and moving his head up and down files and whets his bill, first on one side and then on the other, until he clears the secretion and restores the sense of smell. The Deuteronomy story goes on to say, "As an eagle would do this with their eaglet, so the Lord with His children." Can you see the parallel? Do you need a spiritual overhaul? Do you need to get back on the Right Path?

Teaching those willing to Learn

God the Creator of all living things gives lessons that can teach us how to fly above the storm with the eagles rather than struggle with the turkeys. Young believers must learn to fly by using their own spiritual wings provided by God. They must try. Others will help, but they must try. If the young does not try, they will surely fail. However, if they do their best, they will certainly succeed with the Divine assistance and a little help from their friends. God helps those who help themselves.

Young converts learn to fly through and above the storms of life, while some old believers stop trying and find themselves a secure place, settle in that position, and grow stale and corroded. They lose their appetite for the Word of God and their desire to associate with others. Maturity is a good thing, but aging limits active participation with others and creates problems. Aging at times causes a loss of self worth and lessens the sense of caring for others. This loss includes a weak vision and a dampened spirit of adventure. With these losses, renewal and outreach become the task of others. With a clouded outreach vision, the elderly find themselves a lofty resting place and watch the rest of the world go by. With limited vision and weak nourishment from the Word, aging believers become frail and a set of spiritual illnesses begin to limit their involvement in the faith-based life. As the older ones climb the leadership ladder of a faith-based group, often their spiritual health takes a downward spiral. Unless spiritual renewal occurs, they are lost to the usefulness of the kingdom. Surely, they have a place in heaven, but they will become a liability rather than an asset to the advancement of the gospel unless the youthful spiritual vitality is renewed. In the past the maturing and aging of saints were an asset to the fellowship, because their influence and witness grew stronger.

Healthy Teaching by Seniors

1. But you must speak those things that are appropriate for healthy teaching: 2. charge the senior men to be sober, serious, prudent, healthy in Christian faith and love and endurance. 3. The senior women likewise must behave appropriately for a holy calling, not given to slanderous talk or given to wine, teaching others by good example: 4. in order that they may train the young women to be lovers of their husbands and child lovers, 5. to be sensible, pure, homemakers, good, lining up under the authority of their husbands lest the word of God be abused with foul language. 6. The younger men similarly exhort to be sensible, 7. about all things, showing yourself a pattern of good works in your teaching display purity of motive and seriousness. 8. Present a wholesome message that cannot be criticized; in this way your opponents may be ashamed, having nothing disparaging to say to you. 9. Encourage servants to line up under the authority of their masters and comply with their instructions; not being contentious; 10. not embezzling, but showing loyalty and faithfulness; that they may beautify the teaching of God our Savior in all things. (Titus 2:1-10 EDNT)

When this occurs, God uses different circumstances to bring about creative change. Sometimes God uses other believers or the circumstances of life. At other times, God uses the frailties of the human body as a reality check. With conflict and creative change comes a realization of need to eat again the meat of the Gospel and drink the milk of the Word. Senior believers must continue to grow in grace, but may require extra care and spiritual nourishment by the fellowship. When this occurs, aging believers will eat of the living Word, and find the Rock of Ages where they can pray away their stagnation and spiritual lethargy. By renewing their spiritual youth their interest in spiritual things would revive. Now they will have the spiritual strength to deal with one side of life and then the other until they deal with both the physical and the spiritual problems. They will renew their youth, and then rise above the storms of aging and remain an asset to the fellowship. Scripture declares that believers may run and not grow weary, and walk and not faint; and may renew spiritual youth as the eagle does (Isaiah 40: 31). This will extend the usefulness of aging believers. They have sailed through the storms of life and can become a spiritual beacon to the young by persevering during the final phase of the journey. The eternal victory is worth the battle!

…but he who endures to the end, the same will be saved. (Mark 13:13b EDNT)

16. This is why we are not discouraged; although the outward nature is being worn away, the inner spirit is being refreshed with continual renewal. 17. For our momentary afflictions are a weightless trifle compared to the exceeding and eternal weight of glory; 18. while we fix our gaze on things not seen rather than concentrate on visible things: for the things seen are temporary; but the things not seen are everlasting. (2 Corinthians 4:16-18 EDNT)

CHAPTER FIVE

Checking the Sextant

…for the Lord is my guiding star and safeguards the reading of my sextant to calculate my position and will withhold no good from those who behave with moral integrity. (Psalms 84.11 DOT)

1.… the purpose of this letter is to keep you clear of sin. Meanwhile, if anyone does fall into sin, we have an Advocate to plead our cause before the Father, Jesus Christ the righteous: 2. and He made personal atonement for our sins: but not only concerning our sins, but also all the world. 3. And by this we know that we have known Him, if we keep His commandments. 4. The man who claims knowledge of Him without keeping His commandments is a liar; truth does not dwell in such a man. 5. If a man keeps true to God's word, then it is certain that the love of God has reached its full stature in him; that is what tells us that we are dwelling in God. 6. He who claims that he abides in Him ought himself to live the same kind of life as He lived. 7. Beloved, it is not a new commandment, which I am writing to you, but an old commandment, which you had from the beginning; the old commandment is the word, which you heard. 8. Again, yet it is a new commandment I am sending you, now that it is verified in Him and you; the darkness has passed away now, and true light shines instead. 9. He who claims enlightenment, and all the while hates his brother, is still in darkness. 10. He who loves his brother lives in the light; no fear of stumbling haunts him. 11. The man who hates his brother is in the dark, and takes his steps in the dark without being able to see where he is going; darkness has fallen, and blinded his eyes (1 John 2:1-11 EDNT).

Staying on Course

A sailing ship normally used a sextant to stay on course. There is nothing mystical or complicated about a sextant. The sextant is a navigational instrument used at sea that incorporated a telescope and an angular scale to work out latitude and longitude. Viewing an astronomical object through the telescope and its angular distance above the horizon observed from the scale. This data makes calculating an accurate location possible. A sextant measures the angle between any two visible objects. It was a vital part of celestial navigation during the seafaring age and has some lessons for those who would sail the rough seas of life. The sextant primarily determined the angle between a celestial object and the horizon. With the angle and the time, the viewer could calculate a position line on a nautical chart. Using the sun at high noon or sighting Polaris (known as the Guiding star) at night was essential to staying on a compass course to reach the desired port.

The Spiritual Sextant

A spiritual sextant is the guidance of the Holy Spirit and the words of sacred scripture. The Star of Bethlehem guided Wise men at the birth of Jesus; today the Sun of Righteousness guides believers as promised by Malachi. The Bright and Morning Star, and the illumination of the Spirit on the Word of God becomes a spiritual sextant to assist believers to navigate the challenges of faith-based behavior and stay on course toward the Safe Harbor. This is not an easy task. It takes skill and training to navigate a course by the stars and the horizon. The stars represent heavens light and the horizon represents the future that separates earthly things from heavenly things. By observing both the guiding stars and the distant horizon one can stay on course and keep a proper perspective on the journey.

Continue the Original Course

Location and vocation is the place where called believers serve God and others. Where one lives and what they do determine their personal identity. One might say, "John is a carpenter from Port of Spain;" or "Subesh is a businessman from the village of Plum Mitan." This is how individuals obtain their personal characteristics. Many family names develop because of the father's vocation; for example, since Zimmerman means "carpenter" in German, we can assume Mr. Zimmerman's ancestors were German carpenters. Scripture does not require one to remain in the same location as their birth, but the Word urges believers to remain within the vocation to which they received a call to serve. The new convert has expertise in a vocation and knows the people who can clearly see the changes in lifestyle caused by conversion.

You may remember that the Apostle Paul continued to be a tent maker while he pursued his ministry to the Gentiles. Why was such a restriction necessary? An individual has influence among fellow workers and knows the people. The existing vocation may also be the easiest place to earn a living and take less time from the spiritual mission. This environment is where the Christian witness is the strongest. Seeing changes in lifestyle and behavior is an obvious witness to those who knew them before conversion. When one goes outside their area of influence, it becomes more difficult to reach across the great gulf and witness to strangers. In addition, when one attempts to function in a faith-based group outside their vocational strength, the group may be harmed.

Within one's vocation or trade are valuable lessons and knowledge available in sharing a life changing witness. Jesus told Peter, a working fisher without formal religious training, to use his knowledge of fishing to catch men instead of fish. Jesus said, "From this day forward, you will catch men." By using his fishing experience, Peter immediately had an expertise in how to bring other men to Christ. Jesus used a simple word "catch" meaning "to catch alive." Peter was to catch men alive who would be useful to the kingdom. It is the same for modern converts. They have talent, knowledge, and experience that they can use immediately to advance the Gospel.

> **20. Let each man remain in the calling wherein he was called.** 21. Were you a slave when you believed, stop worrying about it: but if you are made free, live according to your calling in Christ. 22. When a man is called in the Lord being a slave, he is the Lord's freeman: likewise when one is called, being free he becomes Christ's bond-servant. 23. You were bought out of slavery; do not become the servants of men. 24. **Brethren, let each man abide with God where he is called.** (1 Corinthians 7:20-24 EDNT)

The Seeds are in the Fruit

Genesis (1:11) established that the seeds are particular to the fruit. God created within each plant and animal the ability to reproduce itself. This meant that each one would reproduce others of the same kind. The same is true for converts. Within each new believer are seeds of contacts, family members, friends, and colleagues who would accept a witness from a friend filled with tender love and care. Each one knows several individuals who are like seeds with a little friendly cultivation and some spiritual watering could become growing converts within the Christian faith.

> 16 . Do not wander from the right or deviate from the true course, my cherished band of brothers. 17. Every unspoiled and true benefaction is from above, and comes down from the Father of all light, with whom there is no changeableness, neither a dark side where there is no light. 18. Of His own determination procreated as a Father all of us with the expression of genuineness, that we

should be the first matured and collected fruit of God's created beings. (James 1:12-18 EDNT)

Satan's Achilles Heel

The Achilles tendon identifies with one of the greatest warriors of Greek mythology. According to legend, Achilles' mother wanted her son to be immortal, so she dipped the infant into the river Styx. Its sacred waters would make him invincible. But her hand covered his heel, leaving it dry and unprotected. When Achilles went to fight in the Trojan War, an arrow struck the spot—his one weakness—and led to the hero's death.

The Genesis story (3:15) clearly points to Christ bruising the heel of Satan. The Crucifixion was a decisive wound to the heel of Satan's authority over the human race. The Devil seems powerful in many aspects of human life, but the death of Jesus proved to be Satan's downfall.   The Redeeming Messiah struck Satan's Achilles heel and freed the redeemed from the oppression of Satan. This redemption includes all who choose to believe.

That does not mean that Satan has given up, he still attempts to frustrate the lifestyle of believers. Believers must maintain a quiver of arrows to strike at any onslaught of Satan. The Adversary of the Saints knows and believes that Christ is the Son of God and trembles at this know-ledge. Believers must use the arrows of faith against the forces of evil. Consistent faith-based behavior and lifestyle is the best way to withstand evil and overcome wickedness that confronts the moral good in our daily lives.

Jacob grabbing Esau's Heel

The Prophet Hosea (12:3) repeated the construct of Genesis 25:26 when he wrote that Jacob "took his brother by the heel in the womb, and by his strength he had power with God." Jacob wanted to be in position to receive the birthright of the "first born" and grabbed the heel of Esau. When Esau and Jacob (twins) were born, Jacob desiring to be first took hold of Esau's heel; this obvious wound caused Esau later to sell his birthright for a bowl of soup and permitted Jacob to move into the position of the birthright blessing.

Moral Algebra

The word "algebra" means the "reunion of broken parts" and is the study of rules of operations and relations, and the constructions and concepts informed by these rules. A kind of moral algebra is a construct that can enhance an ethical lifestyle, because algebra is a process one learns to solve problems. The rules and guidance in Scripture relative to a moral lifestyle are similar to a moral algebra. There is an algebraic concept in the moral practice of a Christian lifestyle. Basic algebra lessons emphasize the practice or action of understanding the questions and intelligently and simply arriving at the answers. Just as schoolchildren dislike the study of elementary algebra, newly converted Christian are normally reluctant to study the rules and regulations of faith-based behavior. It appears that the immature always want an easy way and are not willing to learn the rules that make life work for the good of all. The "reunion of broken parts" and the study of moral rules of operations and relations, and the constructions and concepts informed by these rules is part of God's design. The Christian experience can put the broken parts of one's life together and once these parts are understood and working by faith a moral lifestyle results.

Examining Lifestyle Regularly by the Word

The Word of God is a measuring stick to determine the quality of one's lifestyle. Believers must daily check their spiritual compass to determine the path they are walking. Is the pathway leading upward toward a positive future or downward toward the valley of temptation? Listening to your heart and clearly understanding the motives that guide your daily life is an important check on the quality of your moral lifestyle. Is your faith-based behavior adequately supporting your witness to family and friends?

Examine your Personal Life

The way one behaves in the family environment sends a message to both family and friends as to their spiritual health. Bad decisions communicate poor judgment and you become a "good bad example" to others. Losing your temper in a difficult situation speaks to your maturity to handle the normal stress of living. A story of a spilled glass of milk illustrates that a problem provides an opportunity to demonstrate mature behavior. It seems a young child spilled his milk and those present waited to see the reaction of the father. The father simply knelt down, put his arm around the child and begin cleaning up the mess but the words were more meaningful than his action. He said to the child, "When I was a little boy I used to spill my milk, too." This was a great comfort to the child and a good example to those present.

Examine your Progress

Growth is always incremental. Progress is always small in comparison to the length of the journey. There are small positive or negative changes in individual lifestyles. The Bible becomes a mirror in which individuals may see themselves the way God sees them. There is always room for improvement and the small steps should come with daily effort to measure behavior in terms of Holy Scripture. Physical and spiritual development is always in phases. The life span of Jesus, illustrates these steps: Jesus grew in, wisdom, stature and favor with God and man. These stages represent mental improvement and physical development, then behavior that is approved by God and socially acceptable to others. Developing the mind and body and a spiritual relationship with God must come before social development. Otherwise, one permits others to bring negative influence on their spiritual life when in reality one's relationship with God is uniquely personal.

> Jesus increased in wisdom and stature, and in favor with God and man (Luke 2:52 EDNT).

Learning to Stay the Course

There are events and the action of others that may push a believer off course. Storms come to every life. The power of the storm does not determine the direction of the ship, it is the decisions one makes about setting the sails. When following the rules, one can take advantage of the force of the storm to move in a forward direction. Knowing the rules and having steadfast endurance are required to stay on course.

Steadfast Endurance

1. Therefore, since we are watched from above by such a cloud of witnesses, let us rid ourselves of all that weighs us down, and the sin that so persistently surrounds us, and **let us run with steadfast endurance, the course that is marked out before us**, 2. Let this fix your eyes on Jesus the origin and the crown of all faith, who, to win his prize of blessedness, endured the cross and made light of its shame, Jesus, who now sits on the right of God's throne. (Hebrews 12:1-2 EDNT)

Enduring hardship is a learning experience; maturity does not come easy. The Old Testament records that human beings are "of a few days and full of trouble." This fact of nature requires all believers to work hard at developing both patience with the human situation and staying power for the journey. The ability to stay the course is a worthy quality of a moral lifestyle. It is important that the positive virtues of spiritual examples be obvious in the behavior and sacred memory of believers. Observing a good example is an encouragement for others to act responsibility.

Lead a Worthy Life

10. You are witnesses and so is God, how upright, honest and blameless was our conduct among you that believe: 11. as you know how we encouraged, comforted, and charged every one of you, as a father treats his children, 12. **that you would lead a life worthy of God, who has called you unto the glory of His kingdom.** (1 Thessalonians 2:10-12 EDNT)

A Workman Unashamed

> 14. Remind them of these things, solemnly witnessing before God not to fight with words, for they are not useful but bring destruction to the ones hearing. 15. **Be eager to present yourself approved to God, a workman unashamed, cutting straight the word of truth.** 16. But avoid blasphemous and worthless chatter: for they will cause more disobeying of the word. (2 Timothy 2:14-19 EDNT)

Absolution and Hope

Someone asked, "Do you believe in rebirth or Reincarnation?" My answer was simply "Yes. As a believer in Jesus I was able to work out arrangements for my afterlife before death." Paul, the Apostle wrote "if a man be in Christ, he is a new creation, old things have passed away and all things have become new."(2 Corinthians 5:17) Therefore, as a believer I began my new life before death and do not have to fret about the rebirth of my soul after death. This New Birth takes place before death and creates a moral lifestyle that brings happiness both to the present human existence and provides hope for the afterlife. The earthly journey remains ahead, but I do not have to concern myself with my afterlife. My relationship with Jesus guarantees my afterlife. I have absolution for the past and hope for the future. Accepting Jesus was a wise choice to eliminate the uncertainty about life after death.

Long-ranged Plans

Developing long-ranged plans keeps one from becoming discouraged with short-term failure or difficulties. When one is clear on a destination, difficulties along the way may only increase the determination to press on to reach the objective.

A story about William Carey is a good example of spiritual perseverance. Many consider Cary as the father of modern missions. He wanted to translate the Bible in many languages and established a print shop where he continually worked on scriptural translations. During an absence, his print shop burned with the loss of years of labor. The loss included his extensive library, grammar books and translation manuscripts, and many reams of print paper. Hearing of the fire Carey said, "The work of years gone in a moment."

Carey had no time for mourning, he went to work rebuilding saying, "We were cast down but not in despair." When news of the fire reached England, funds and volunteers came to help. Rebuilding the print shop increased the production of Bibles, New Testaments, or books of scripture printed in forty-four languages. Carey's attitude was "We must go forward."

Constant Prayer for Worthy Behavior

> 9. For this purpose, since the day we heard it, we have not ceased to pray for you and to desire that you might be filled with the knowledge of His will in all wisdom and spiritual understanding; 10. that you might **behave worthy of the pleasing of the Lord**, personally bearing good fruit and increasing in the full knowledge of God; 11. being empowered according to His glorious power, with a cheerful exercise of endurance and unlimited perseverance; 12. joyously giving thanks to the Father, who made us sufficient to partake of the inheritance of the saints who live in the light: 13. who has rescued us from the dominion of darkness, and has transformed us into the kingdom of His dear Son: 14. in whom we have redemption through His blood, even the forgiveness of sins: (Colossians 1:9-14 EDNT).

CHAPTER SIX

Keeping the Logbook

2. You are our letter of recommendation written in our hearts, known and read of all men: 3. you are an open letter from Christ transcribed by us, written not with ink, but with the Spirit of the living God; not on tables of stone, but on pages of the human heart. (2 Corinthians 3:2 EDNT)

A Legal Document

Keeping a detail log of all events and orders was central to the operation of a sailing ship. The logbook was a legal document and the record could justify actions in court or condemn and convict those who violated the standard orders of the Ship's Captain or failed to act properly under all circumstances. The logbook was both the evidence of crew behavior and the official record of the ships journey including origination and destination. The names of the officers and crew, the specified cargo manifest, notations of changing weather, and all the difficulties with the crew and the ship were timely recorded in the logbook.

A Historical Record

The Book of Acts was a historical record of the first thirty years of the New Testament journey identifying the activities of the earliest believers. It was a record of how the Holy

Spirit worked through individuals and how Satan used some people in an attempt to hinder the growth and development of the moral cause. The behavior of the disciples enabled by the power of the Holy Spirit brought about change in the people they daily encountered. It recorded both good and bad behavior.

In Acts, Luke records the outpouring of the Spirit on obedient followers. They were obeying the instructions of Jesus to wait in Jerusalem expectantly for the Holy Spirit before they continued their journey as witnesses to the known world. Acts records the fear and doubt of some followers and the boldness and fearlessness of others. Luke records the good and bad of a struggling body of believers as they endeavored to establish houses of faith and do missionary work in their effort to make new disciples. Some rejected their witness and persecuted them for their beliefs, but they continued with the aid of the Spirit to obey the command of Jesus to "make disciples." The Lord added to their number daily, but some rejected the message of salvation. Some tried to purchase the power of God, others attempted to place personal conditions on following the messengers on their faith-based path to eternal life. All that was required was simple faith in the message, together with a willingness to obey the rules of Jesus and follow the guidance of the Holy Spirit. Yet, some resisted the Jesus Way; it was their loss.

18. When Simon saw that the Spirit was bestowed by the laying on of the apostles' hands, he offered them money. 19. Saying, Give me this authority, so that when I lay hands on someone, he receives the Holy Spirit. 20. But Peter said, Your money disappear with you, because you thought the gift of God could be purchased with money. 21. **You have no part or share in this ministry: for your heart is not right with God. 22. Repent of your wrong doings and pray, if perhaps the thought of your heart may be forgiven. 23. For I recognize that you are enraged with bitterness and are a slave to wickedness.** 24. Then

Simon replied, Pray to the Lord for me that none of these things that you have spoken will come upon me. (Acts 8: 18-24 EDNT)

An Example

Others hesitated and resisted but later accepted the call of Jesus. One example was Saul of Tarsus, a strict Jew, who persecuted all who followed Jesus, but saw the light on the way to Damascus and went to Straight Street and received guidance to believe, and became a strong follower of Jesus. The Apostle Paul wrote one-fourth of the New Testament. Between Luke, a Gentile Physician, and Paul, a Jewish convert, God entrusted them to write one-half of the New Testament. This alone demonstrates the great power of forgiveness and the enabling of the Holy Spirit that is now available to all who will accept Jesus as the Redeemer sent from God! One should never diminish education because Paul and Luke were both educated professionals. God also used a rough and salty boatman, know as Peter, to advance the gospel. Jesus even chose a tax collector as part of the original twelve who were learning to follow the Right Path. The diversity of those who followed Jesus is an important part of the message of grace and forgiveness. Mercy and forgiveness were open to all willing to follow in faith the footsteps of Jesus.

Behave with Wisdom

5. Behave with wisdom toward non-Christians, buying up every opportunity. 6. Always make your speech pleasing and tasteful, that you may know how to give a proper answer to every question. (Colossians 4:5-6 EDNT).

A Written Record of Blessings

My firm conviction is that each believer should write down every blessing from God including answers to prayers and effective witnessing episodes. If individuals would keep a written journal of God's dealing with them, their family, friends, such a journal would read similar to a chapter in the

Book of Acts. An available record of God's intervention in their personal lives, answered prayers, spiritual enablement for special tasks, and the general working of the Holy Spirit in their life could become a stronghold and source of encouragement during difficult times. Having a personal journal to remind one of God's blessings would create stamina to continue through the normal difficulties of life. Memories usually fade with time and a written record would refresh the recollection of God's past blessings and encourage one on their moral and faith-based journey regardless of the difficulties.

It would be wonderful if individuals kept a personal record of God's intervention in their private lives. During times of difficulty, the reading of such a logbook would be a source of spiritual encouragement. It would have been a great loss if early believers had not recorded the events of their spiritual journey that are now in the Bible. What if the history of Israel's journey out of Egypt to the Promise Land were omitted from the sacred writings? What if there were no records of God's dealing with early believers in the Book of Acts? What if the Promises of God were not recorded for the benefit of others? These are wonderful and meaningful memories with great spiritual value. They become a bridge over the troubled waters of human existence.

Meaningful Memories

Recording blessings and answered prayers is important. This would be behavior making a personal record similar to a chapter in Acts and would record meaningful memories. Paul remembered important aspects of converts in Thessalonians. He recalled the time when faith began to work in their lives that caused them to turn to God from idols. Paul remembered that the love for God produced physical labor and prompted true serviced to the living and true God. He committed to memory their enduring patience that produced hope and a willingness to wait for the return of the Risen Lord (1 Thessalonians 1:2-10).

Neglect of Beneficial Activities

In the hurry-worry of modern society, it seems that daily activities and business crowds out many beneficial activities. Not only is there a neglect to record meaningful memories there is disregard for personal and systematic study of the Word as well as the benefits of personal prayers. An emptiness is created by a life busy doing "things" and seeking personal pleasure rather than using the calm and comfort of prayer and study of the Word of God. Why did God preserve the written record of His dealing with the human race from the Creation to the Revelation of Jesus Christ to John? This was done for the benefit of believers, but we have to avail ourselves of the printed word we call the Bible. Reading the Bible mixed with personal prayer enables a clear understanding and application to the daily situations of life. There is no better guide book.

Develop a Mindset and Dedication

Believers should develop a new mindset and dedication that brings a commitment to self-discipline in Bible study, prayer, worship attendance, and daily lifestyle witness. Devotional Bible study is a good start, because reading the Word of God will prompt personal prayer and provide guidance for a lifestyle of moral behavior. Here are seven steps to enhance the reading sacred scripture:

1. Mediate a moment in prayer to clear the mind and then read with an honest desire to receive what God is saying.

2. Seek to receive what the Scripture means and apply it to the personal situations in your life

3. As you prayerfully read the passage (paragraph), depend on the Holy Spirit to illuminate the true meaning and enable you to apply the passage to your personal life.

4. Permit the passage to bring to mind concerns for prayer. Write down those concerns and include them in your daily prayers.

5. Allow the Holy Spirit to guide you in bringing your life into spiritual compliance with the Word.

6. Let the Word speak directly to you, your family, your work, and personal life situation.

7. After reading the Word, pray for the Holy Spirit to use the Word in your life to ensure spiritual growth. Share what you have learned with someone, anyone who will listen. If there is no one around to hear, write a note, send an email, phone someone and share what you have learned.

The Kernel of Life Lost

Jesus shared a parable about how the kernel of life in the Word could be so easily lost. Lost because the ground was not prepared or the essential truth was not cultivated or watered. It was clear that the "seed" was the Word of God. Reading or listening is not enough unless the individual nourishes the truth learned from the reading. A broken spirit that brings tears in prayer can water the word to grow in the heart of a sincere believer.

> 5. A farmer went out to sow his seed: and as he sowed, some seeds fell beside the footpath; and it was walked on, and the birds consumed it. 6. And some fell on rocky ground; and as soon as it came up, it withered away, because it lacked moisture. 7. And some fell among prickly weeds; and the thistles sprang up with it, and choked it. 8. And other seeds fell on good ground, and sprang up, and produced fruit a hundredfold. And when He had said these things, He cried, He that has ears to hear let him listen. (Luke 8: 5-8 EDNT)

To concentrate on what you read and be able to express clearly and precisely the understanding is crucial to reading scripture. It may be acceptable to have an unsystematic approach to the reading of other books, but a haphazard attitude is not suitable when approaching the Word of God. One must read God's Word with both attention and respect. A proper approach to the Bible can rule out the flawed thinking of others as one pursues the true meaning of scripture. Constant attention is required when one wishes to understand the meaning of scripture. It is reasonable to conclude that personal and systematic reading of scripture is a valuable asset to faith-based behavior and a moral lifestyle.

Serious Business

Reading the Bible is serious business. It should be a disciplined and controlled process. Personal prayer enhances the soundness of the understanding and strengthens the lessons learned from scripture. This is a learned behavior and with regular use will be meaningful to the reader. The ability to approach the Bible with respect and clear thinking helps to filter out the flawed thinking of others. Applying the understanding to the personal life of the reader, the Word becomes a usable guide to establish a moral lifestyle.

Evening and Morning Meditation

Paul wrote about a regular conversation with God as a believer's daily renewal. This is why we are never discouraged; although the outward nature is being worn away, the inner life is being refreshed from day to day (2 Corinthians 4:16 EDNT). Honest conversation with God comes in regular evening and morning devotions that include both the reading of scripture and engaging in the silent side of prayer; that is the listening side, where one prays and patiently waits for God to provide a clear answer.

There is a present need for daily devotional reading and personal study of the New Testament. Attending a worship service, with all the benefits, is not sufficient for daily growth and development of the individual believer. Much of the value for the individual is lost in the programming for institutional advance. Most existing translations and versions of the New Testament are overly academic and have little devotional value for the average reader. This is why I recommend a common language version for devotional reading arranged in chronological order by books.

Evening and Morning Readings

Why do we suggest that the reading be done first in the evening and then in the morning? Genesis declared "And the evening and the morning were the first day." This continued for each day of Creation and established that the evening before the daylight goes with the next light. The Jewish religion recognized this and began the Sabbath on Friday evening at sundown until sundown the next day. Although the Resurrection of Christ of the First Day of the Week influenced the followers of Christ to worship on Sunday rather than Saturday, the pattern was clear. The slave culture of the day forced over one-half of the people into servitude, yet they could worship in the evening (Saturday) at sundown which in reality was the beginning of the first day of the week. Remember, Jesus was resurrected when it was yet dark, the evening that goes with the First Day.

Although the modern church has lost the real impact of the "First day punch" the reality of an "evening and morning" reading and study plan could take one back to a fundamental understanding of the Creator's master plan. To wait until the morning to begin devotions is to lose the "sundown to sunup portion of the day." A full discussion of this issue may be found in chapter one of *Why Churches Die* listed in the references and in the notes of *The EVERGREEN Devotional New Testament*.

A systematic reading of the Bible is important. The evening is the time to prepare for the day. The habit of thinking differently about the day is not easy to form or to maintain, but it is most rewarding — even priceless! A daily quiet time, which promotes regular reading of the Word in a general chronological pattern, will be an encouragement to spirituality. Write down the things you learn and then use them in your life.

Structured Scripture Reading

Structured scripture reading twice a day, evening and morning, that takes the reader through the New Testament at a regular pace. Each session should range from ten (10) to thirty (30) minutes depending on the seriousness of the study suggested in the paragraph (expository unit) read. Those who have more time are encouraged to spend additional time in study and prayer. Then listen for God for a clear answer.

Divided into Expository Units

This book includes a guide to read the New Testament book by book in evening and morning units in a general chronological order. Why use this order? Genesis was clear "the evening and morning" were the parameter of the day. A chronological order of reading the New Testament improves the understanding of God's progressive dealing with the human race and enables one to see the process as a direct benefit for today. The evening and morning recommendation is to place the reader in a creative atmosphere for renewal. Since it is obvious that the scriptures came over time and that no writer received all of God's special revelation at once, it is logical to assume that each writer was progressive in the expression of the revelation; consequently, the work of each writer should be read chronologically in turn to see clearly this progression.

1. Are we beginning afresh to recommend ourselves? Or do we need as others, letters of commendation to you or recommendation letters from you? 2. You are our letter of recommendation written in our hearts, known and read of all men: 3. **you are an open letter from Christ transcribed by us, written not with ink, but with the Spirit of the living God; not on tables of stone, but on pages of the human heart.** 4. Such pure confidence

we have through Christ toward God: 5. not that we were sufficiently qualified ourselves, but our sufficiency comes from the Sufficient One; 6. who also made us ministers of the new covenant; not with letters of the alphabet, but of the spirit: the letter of the law punishes with death, but the Spirit gives life to the soul. (2 Corinthians 3:1-11 EDNT)

Record of Evening and Morning Reading

You may keep a record of your reading by circling the Chapter numbers as they are completed. This is important should you skip around because of an interest in a particular passage based on what you heard in church, on TV, etc. Always keep in mind both the human writer of the passage and the inspiration of the Holy Spirit that prompted and motivated the writing of the words. There were eight (8) human writers of the New Testament; however, the Holy Spirit was the true Author. Peter wrote about this (2 Peter 1:21).

The writer is marked after the name of the Book or Letter. The code for writers is:

- [J] James;
- [JD] John, the Disciple;
- [JJB] Jude, Jesus' Brother;
- [JM] John Mark;
- [L] Luke;
- [M] Matthew;
- [P] Paul;
- [SP] Simon Peter.

Order and Record of Chronological Reading

Book	Writer	Chapters
James	[J]	1 2 3 4 5
Mark	[JM]	1 2 3 4 5 6 7 8 9 10 11 12 13 14 15 16
I Thessalonians	[P]	1 2 3 4 5
II Thessalonians	[P]	1 2 3
Galatians	[P]	1 2 3 4 5 6
I Corinthians	[P]	1 2 3 4 5 6 7 8 9 10 11 12 13 14 15 16
II Corinthians	[P]	1 2 3 4 5 6 7 8 9 10 11 12 13
Romans	[P]	1 2 3 4 5 6 7 8 9 10 11 12 13 14 15 16
Luke	[L]	1 2 3 4 5 6 7 8 9 10 11 12 13 14 15 16 17 18 19 20 21 22 23 24
Matthew	[M]	1 2 3 4 5 6 7 8 9 10 11 12 13 14 15 16 17 18 19 20 21 22 23 24 25 26 27 28
Philemon	[P]	1
Colossians	[P]	1 2 3 4
Ephesians	[P]	1 2 3 4 5 6
Philippians	[P]	1 2 3 4
Acts	[L]	1 2 3 4 5 6 7 8 9 10 11 12 13 14 15 16 17 18 19 20 21 22 23 24 25 26 27 28
I Timothy	[P]	1 2 3 4 5 6
Titus	[P]	1 2 3
II Timothy	[P]	1 2 3 4
I Peter	[SP]	1 2 3 4 5
Jude	[JJB]	1
Hebrews	[P]	1 2 3 4 5 6 7 8 9 10 11 12 13
II Peter	[SP]	1 2 3
John	[JD]	1 2 3 4 5 6 7 8 9 10 11 12 13 14 15 16 17 18 19 20 21
I John	[JD]	1 2 3 4 5
II John	[JD]	1
III John	[JD]	1
Revelation	[JD]	1 2 3 4 5 6 7 8 9 10 11 12 13 14 15 16 17 18 19 20 21 22

Lifestyle Evangelism

Lifestyle evangelism is akin to friendship evangelism based on fellowship that includes affability, association, or affiliation. This kind of fellowship is reality two fellows in the same ship and it must not be a warship. True soul-winning evangelism is reaching an individual at their point of need at the earliest point in time at a considerable distance from a church building; in other words, in the marketplace or on common ground. The best way to share the good news is with those with whom one has common interests, goals, views, or experiences.

Entrenched and Growing in Christ

6. Since you received Christ Jesus the Lord, so behave in union with Him. 7. Entrenched and growing in Christ, confirmed in faith, as you were taught, flourishing in faith with thanksgiving. 8. Be cautious lest any man stain you through a flawed viewpoint and worthless deception, after human tradition, after the basics of the world, and not after Christ. 9. For in Him the fullness of the Godhead dwells incarnate. 10. And you are complete in Christ, who is the head of all authorities and powers: 11. In whom you wholly put away from yourself the sins of the flesh without hands by a spiritual operation of Christ: 12. Covered with Him in baptism, wherein you were raised with Him through faith in the operation of God, who stood Christ up from the grave. (Colossians 2:6-12 EDNT)

The Right Angle Encounter

7. But if we walk in the light, as He is in the light, we have fellowship one with another, and the blood of Jesus Christ His Son cleanses us from all sin. (1 John 1:7 EDNT)

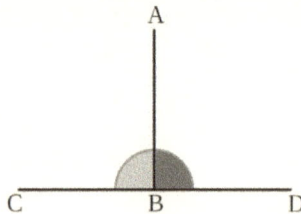

The verse above (1 John 1:7) illustrates the right angle relationships that exist when a believer is in fellowship with God (A-B), and the right angle or vertical connection between the heart of man and the heart of God is established. When the right angle encounter is working, the believer has the wisdom and power to reach both backward (B-C) for fellowship with family and friends and forward (B-D) in service to God and witness to others.

> 17. Whereas the wisdom that comes from above is marked by purity, then peacefulness; it is courteous and ready to be convinced, always taking the better part, It carries mercy with it and is a harvest of all that is good, undivided in mind, without hypocrisy. 18. Peace is the seed-ground of righteousness, and those who make peace will reap the harvest. (James 3:17 EDNT)

Who are you in Luke's Story?

Does your culture or religion restrict you from assisting a stranger in need? When it comes to helping a stranger, you have a choice. Whom do you choose to be in this story: the Priest, the Levite, or the Samaritan? It is the parable about a hated half-breed who acted responsibly while religious leaders refused to assist a wounded man. It is a story of individual choice on the part of one and a religious cop-out by two others.

The story filled with scandal, is one of the most frequently told parables in the Holy Scripture. The story presented in a Jewish context but recorded only in the Gospel of Luke written by a Gentile. Luke wrote the Gospel for a Roman to point out the contract between Caesar, a mortal man claiming to be a god, and Jesus, the God who became man.

> 30. And Jesus said, a man on his way to Jericho from Jerusalem fell among bandits, who took his cloths and beat him and left him half dead. 31. By chance a priest passed that way: and when he saw him passed by on the other side, 32, and by chance a Levite, came to the scene, looked and passed by on the other side. 33. But a Samaritan on his journey came and saw him and had compassion on him, 34. and went to him, dressed his wounds, using oil and wine and put him on his own donkey and took him to an inn and cared for him. 35. And when he departed the next day, he gave the innkeeper

some money and said, Take care of him and if it cost more when I return I will pay. 36. Which of these three do you think was neighbor to the man who fell among bandits? 37. And he answered, The one who showed compassion. Then Jesus said, **Go and do the same for others.** (Luke 10:29b-37 EDNT)

It seems that Jesus chose a hated half-breed to be the hero and demonstrate how some because of religion or culture avoid responsibility. The Jewish ceremonial law of cleanliness prohibited the touching of a dead body; therefore, to assume a wounded stranger was dead gave them a defendable pass. Yet, the Samaritan, most likely a traveling salesman, had no such religious or cultural narrow-mindedness. The wounded man in the ditch could be a past or future customer. At least, he was a human being in trouble and needed assistance, and the Samaritan felt neighborly. Often we find an excuse to avoid assisting the needy, when the opportunity to be a good neighbor is present.

Who are you to pass judgment on others near to you? 13. See how you say, today or tomorrow we will go to such a city, work there for a year, trade and make a profit. 14. When you have no means of knowing what tomorrow will bring. What is your life? It is a mist that appears and soon vanishes. 15. What you should say, If the Lord will, we shall live, and do this or that. 16. But your arrogant ways make boasters of you: all such bragging is wickedness. 17. **Therefore, if a man has the power to do good; and fails to do good it is sinful.** (James 4: 12b-17 EDNT)

Reflecting His Love to the World Around

Remembering incidents when God enabled me to share the message of grace with others or when others shared with me becomes a window that lets me see into God's own heart. The Lord has poured down blessings upon us through so many amazing people that we must continue to share with the blessings of Christ with others   In my journey as a Christian, God has used many opportunities to teach me to think and love as He does. These opportunities have come in different shapes and sizes, many disguised as problems, challenges and inconveniences. However, in each case, God has showed His love, care and compassion for others.

Meeting with the Jewish Carpenter

On a flight to Miami, my wife and I observed a flight attendant who looked physically fit. My wife was involved in a personal nutrition and exercise plan, so we began our conversation there. As we shared about our work with abandoned, disadvantaged and children of misfortune, we saw her pained expression. Sharing about the loss of her son, a medical intern, to an overdose of drugs, she blamed his roommate. As a result, she was overcome with resentment and hate for the young man. Arranging for a "first class" place to chat, we prayed with her that God would heal her hurt and help her to forgive. She was Jewish and I asked if I could introduce her to the Jewish Carpenter, Jesus Christ. She consented and she invited Christ into her life as a personal Saviour. Jesus, speaking about loving one another, fruitful prayers, and the rules about sharing faith, made it clear that gaining converts (fruit) alone was not sufficient "that your fruit should remain." Consequently, we put this new convert in touch with friends in New Your City who could assist her along her journey of understanding, knowing and walking with God.

> 16. You have not chosen me, but I have chosen you, and appointed you to **go out and bring in fruit**, and **that your fruit should remain**: and that you should **obtain answers to your prayers to make them fruitful.** 17. These things I command you, so that you may **love one another.** (John 15 16-17 EDNT)

Forgiveness in a Bag

While visiting in Miami, someone broke into the trunk of a parked car and took our bag and valuables. Debbie and I prayed for the return of the bag and that God would forgive those involved in the robbery. We prayed that they would come to know Jesus as a personal Saviour. Shortly after the prayer, someone called our hotel and said that he had found the bag with our contact information. He also told us he had seen a Bible in the bag and thought it must belong to "a servant of God." He returned the bag to us with everything in it – nothing was missing. Realizing that God was not only concerned about us, but about those who had wronged us. Evidently, God wanted us to forgive and express concern for those who took the things that belonged to us. It became clear that forgiveness was a good foundation for a fruitful prayer. James 5:16 makes it clear there I great power in the fervent prayer of the righteous. Believers should never underestimate the power of a sincere prayer.

Building Families One Brick at a Time

One of the basic needs as human beings is proper housing. We have been involved in several projects to make housing options available at an affordable cost to individuals and families. We provided financial assistance and technical direction to help construct a home for a needy family in Las Lomas. In addition to providing technical advice and assistance to several families as they undertook home construction projects, in the Anapausis Community, we have built housing-units and provided interest free loans to families to help them purchase homes. Anapausis has provided housing for a Law student from the University of the West Indies for three (3) years while she pursued her Law degree. Anapausis has provided shelter and apartments for several young people coming out of custodial care at the Bridge of Hope. One never loses a blessing while blessing others. This is always true whether we recognize it or not. At times, God may delay the return on a blessing investment, but as the old preacher said, "Cast your bread on the water and it will come back spread with butter and jam." God keeps good records.

Providing a Bridge of Hope

The ministry of the Anapausis Community, the childcare

at the Bridge of Hope, and the personal ministry of me and my wife, deals with all ages of people. We are concerned about the quality of life for each individual regardless of age and are particularly concerned about the empowerment of couples to live a quality life. However, a particular burden developed in a vision for Bridge of Hope that included not only a capacity for basic childcare, but also residential quarters for needy children. Reaching and caring for underprivileged and the orphan is part of the ministry of the Bridge of Hope. This aspect of our ministry has been in operation along the Eastern seaboard of Trinidad since 1998 and has changed the standard of living for some of the most needy. Bridge of Hope grew out of a theology of the disadvantaged and produced and a safe place for abused, abandoned, and disadvantaged children to grow, develop and bloom into productive citizens. Among the positive outcomes is the shining light of Bisham (Rakesh) Ramkisson. Here is his personal story.

> I was born into a Hindu family in a village called Ecclesville deep in south Trinidad where life was not easy for his family. Living with an abusive, drug addict and alcoholic father, his two younger brothers continuously struggled with daily challenges. Constant abuse caused Rakesh's mother to run out of the mess and chaos in the middle of the night leaving behind three children ages 1, 3 and 4. Considering the state the father, who was addicted to drugs and alcohol, the children were practically abandoned. The little money earned from farming, the father invested into Marijuana and Bay Rum leaving the children without food and deprived of an education.

> I lived each day on the street surviving on mangos from my grandmother's mango tree as the main source of food and for the days that mangos were out of season, I would walk out to the main village begging for something to eat. Looking back at it all, I now truly understand what the Lord meant when he said that he would be the father to the fatherless and the mother to the motherless.

At the age of 6, I found myself running missions for my father, having to walk about a mile and half from home to collect packages. One day on my way back home, despite being warned "don't open the bag," I opened to see what was inside. In the bag was a foil paper with dried leaves, not knowing what it was I dumped everything in the bushes and went home thinking I did the right thing, and told my father that all I got was dried grass. Well, he flogged me with everything he found in his way, wooden brooms, kitchen spoons and curtain rods.

This continued for two more years until my aunt got the police involved. She created a lie, telling the police that we were being sexually abused by my father. After the officers were finished with their investigation, we were brought down to the station. I remember see my father at the station cry "tell them the truth" and the officers would hit him every time he tried defending himself. So, my brothers and I were taken to court and then transferred to Bridge of Hope and my father was sent to prison.

Early life at Bridge of Hope was rough. Having to adjust to a new lifestyle with a much bigger family proved a bit difficult, but with time everything fell into place. At Bridge of Hope, I was introduced to Christ. Understood that everything had happen for a purpose and that God was in control. My life began turning around and I started school at the age of 8 in preschool until I was able to quickly pick up and skip ahead to a class with my age group. Pushing through, I completed primary school and moved on to high school where I finished with seven O'Level subjects and awards for Conduct.

I am currently employed with a successful company gaining hands on knowledge and experience on the key aspects of business management, purchasing and inventory control. With the blessings of the Lord, I was able to purchase my own apartment and God has now blessed me with a brand new car. I am and will always be grateful for His intervention in my life, living each day understanding the promise He gave to me: "For I know the plans I have for you," declares the Lord, "plans to prosper

you and not to harm you, plans to give you hope and a
future." Jeremiah 29:11. --(Rakesh) Ramkisson

Helping Children Climb the Ladder

The Anapausis Society set up a fund dedicated to helping young people further their education and development.
The Society recently gave its first scholarship to Jonathan
Gosyne as he left for Georgia Tech University in Atlanta, to
pursue a degree in Mathematics. Jonathan scored a perfect
score on the National Math Exam and received a National
Scholarship, but it did not fully fund his expenses. The
Anapausis Society was pleased to bless this bright young
man on his journey to a quality education and a hopeful
future.

The Power of Positive Thinking

Every meeting is an opportunity to share positive concepts with others. Entering the office of a medical doctor,
I saw on his desk a book, The Power of Positive Thinking by
Norman Vincent Peale. Aware of the content of the book,
I engaged him in a discussion on the principles of positive
thinking. From this, four other discussions followed during
which he invited Christ into his life as a personal Saviour. As
a Financial Consultant, I am now assisting him on a hospital
building project. Recently, this man decided to commit
personal funds to assist with another worthy project. It is
wonderful how God works in both directions. It appears
that the Malachi 3:8-12 blessing that opens the "windows of
heaven" to bless those who share, worked in this situation.
God is good!

A Personal Sacrifice can Fill a Void

Elena, a cruise ship Hostess, was a friendly Lady. We were
pleased to meet her. At Elena's request, Debbie and I began
sharing about ourselves. She asked to talk with us when she
had more time. We made ourselves available on her day off
to continue the conversation. This was a personal sacrifice
since we chose to meet with her instead of going off ship for

a day trip. Elena shared her personal story: in order to work and help provide for her family, she was apart from both her daughter and the man she loved. This separation created a huge void in her life. Offering to pray with her, Elena embraced the opportunity and invited Jesus into her life as a personal Saviour. She was so excited about this personal encounter with Jesus that she shared her experience with her roommate. God works wonders when one shares both burdens and blessings even on a cruise ship. An old saying gets to the heart of the matter, **a burden shared is half as heavy; a blessing shared is twice as nice!**

Building an Environment and Community for the Elderly

At present, we are building Olive's House in Sangre Chiquito, Trinidad, a four-stage project for the Elderly. One of the most prominent needs of the elderly, apart from proper physical care, is for meaningful interaction with others so they can pass on their acquired wisdom and the lessons learned in their life to the next generation. Olive's House is next to the Bridge of Hope, a childcare centre and Olive's House provides opportunity for the children to associate with older adults. The elderly who lack daily visits from their own children and grandchildren are pleased with the opportunity for involvement with the children. Since child/adult association is a major void in their lives, the elderly become surrogate grandparents and are able to share with the children missing elements of their childhood. Olive's House becomes a double blessing: the children have access to surrogate grandparents and the Elderly have the blessing of sharing with the children.

Partnership with Urban India Ministries

Urban India Ministries (UIM) pioneer and director Dr. P.C. Matthews recently visited Trinidad. On seeing Bridge of Hope, the Children's Home in Sangre Chiquito, he was challenged to begin work in a slum village, LR Nagar in India. This village is home to over 1,000 families and he has agreed to take the Bridge of Hope Model and the lessons learned to this Indian community. Already Dr. Matthews has acquired one staff, who grew up in such a community and understands the need and is willing to lead the charge to establish a Bridge of Hope in India. It is wonderful how God works to expand His love and care for needy children.

An Encouragement to Other Leaders

On his visit to Trinidad, I took Dr. P. C. Matthews of Urban India Ministries (UIM), to meet with business leaders who might be interested in assisting his efforts to reach the poor and needy in India. The local leaders showed not only interest in the needs of India, but provided immediate assistance to the project. Also, on a visit to pray with a couple about their situation, I took Dr. Matthews. This couple was of another faith. We prayed with them in the Name of Jesus. Dr. Matthews was encouraged that we could visit and pray with persons of other faiths and see real results. This together with the assistance of the local business leaders proved to be a great encouragement to his work in India.

Learning Lessons from each Encounter

1. We must embrace each and every ministry opportunities.

2. We must view people and their situations through the eyes of love and compassion.

3. While you may not personally be able to meet a need, do not break the link with the one in need. Always attempt to connect him/her to those who can assist with the need.

4. Proper stewardship of current responsibilities is essential in order to pass on the lessons you have learned.

5. Always turn what you do not need into a seed.

6. When you work with others God has a way of growing the seeds you plant.

7.   God's harvest is far beyond your expectation.

Knocking Holes in the Darkness

There is a story about an old man who seemed to "knock holes in the darkness" of an early New England town. He was the town Lamplighter. In the early evening, he would go street by street and light the gas lamps on each corner. The old gas lamps were dim but made a small light on the dark street. As the old Lamplighter went from street to street, it appeared that he was knocking holes in the darkness. He made his world a little brighter. This is a good example for believers. Have you knocked any holes in the darkness in your neighborhood? Have you made the night a little brighter in your community? Let your light shine; you can make a difference!

Important Facts

The believers in Berea were good examples because they "were eager to receive the word and search daily the scriptures to verify what was said" (Acts 17:11 EDNT). A few important facts:

1. The deep things of God are revealed by the Spirit:

9. Written in scripture, eye has not seen, nor ear heard, neither has entered into the heart of man, the things that God has prepared for those who love Him. 10. But God has unveiled them to us by His Spirit: for the Spirit searches all things, and affirms the deep things of God. 11. For what human being can know the thoughts of a man, save the spirit of man which is in him? Even so no man knows the things of God, but the Spirit of God. 12. We have not received the spirit of the world, but the Spirit that is of God; that we might know the things that are freely given to us by God. 13. We do not speak of these things in language taught by men, but that which the Holy Spirit teaches; explaining spiritual things in spiritual words. 14. The natural man does not accept the things of the Spirit of God: for they are nonsense to him: they just do not make sense to him: neither can he understand them, because

they are only discerned spiritually (1 Corinthians 1: 9-14 EDNT).

2. The teaching ministry of the Holy Spirit is not available to the unconverted:

14. The natural man does not accept the things of the Spirit of God: for they are nonsense to him: they just do not make sense to him: neither can he understand them, because they are only discerned spiritually. 15. But the man with spiritual insight can judge the worth of everything, yet no one can give an informed judgment of him. 16. For who knows the mind of the Lord, that he may instruct him? But we have the mind of Christ (1 Corinthians 2:14-16 EDNT).

3. A carnal or unspiritual person will not come to the fullness of spiritual truth:

1. Brethren, I could not speak to you as unto spiritually mature men, but as to men with carnal appetites, even as infant Christians. 2. I gave you spiritual milk and not solid teachings: for until then you were not able to digest strong teaching, nor are you able even now. 3. For you are yet self-sufficient without dependence on God: because there is among you strife, jealousy and party feelings, are you not still controlled by your own nature, and behave as the unconverted (1 Corinthians 3:1-3 EDNT).

4. Truth requires believing and believing requires behaving. The admonition is to hear and do:

22. You must be honest with yourselves and live by the word not merely hear it. 23. But if any man listens to the word, and does not behave it, he is similar to a man seeing his own face in a mirror; 24. He observes his flaws, and immediately forgets the man he saw. 25. But whosoever bows down to observe the complete prescriptive usage and the unrestrained opportunity to continue in the word and not become a forgetful hearer, but one who behaves the prescribed deeds, this man shall by the blood be set apart for consecrated action. 26. If any man among you seem to be devout, and restrains not his unnatural

language, he deceives his own heart and his service to
God is ineffective (James 1:22-25 EDNT).

5. Spiritual obedience includes believing and behaving:

You are my friends, if you do whatever I command you
(John 15:14 EDNT).

**6. Truth demands obedience. The Bible becomes a
closed book to those who persist in disobedience:**

And Jesus continued, Is a lamp put under a bushel, or
under a bed? And not to be placed on a lamp-stand?
22. For there is nothing hid, except it will be manifested;
neither is anything concealed, except it will be revealed.
23. If anyone has ears to hear, let him listen. 24. Then he
added, Take care how you listen: with what gauge you
use to measure, it shall be calculated to you: and to you
who listens, more shall be added to you. 25. For he who
has, shall be given more: and he who holds back shall be
deprived of what he has (Mark 4:21-25 EDNT).

Spiritual Autism (SA)

Autism in children is a complicated disorder, as regarding
its treatment, diagnosis, and causes. An application of
autism symptoms checklist to new converts could suggest
certain similarities in the development of converts in their
becoming a productive believer. Some behavioral patterns
commonly seen in autistic children could assist the problem-
solving process in the developmental patterns in the lifestyle
of new believers.

1. Spiritual Autistic difficulties may strike early in the
life of a new convert. Unclear symptoms make the
problem-solving process difficult. With weak follow-
up of new converts, the flaws in their development
are often overlooked. Perhaps faith-based groups
should develop a Behavior Checklist for Believers and
regularly apply it to new converts.

2. The main difficulty for such a Behavior Checklist is
the negative recognition of the weakness without a

spiritual process to improve behavior of the convert.

3. Mature Christians must spend more time and energy on nurturing new converts. A primary task of the followers of Jesus was to "make disciples" not just bring them to conversion. This was done by lifestyle evangelism that included a process of identification with the Trinity through baptism and a program for teaching new disciples about the expected lifestyle of believers.

4. New converts may be unconcerned about the dangers of the world and may continue associations and activities that will hinder their growth in grace and knowledge of a faith-based lifestyle.

5. Those with spiritual autism may not desire to cooperate with others or participate in group activities that are essential to their spiritual development.

6. Converts with spiritual autism may have a spiritual "fellowship" deficiency.

7. Spiritual autism produces bad temper and a non-cooperative spirit related to others. They may be unable to respond well toward witnessing to others.

8. Such non-social attitudes cause those with spiritual autism to develop selfish behavior.

9. New converts who suffer from spiritual autism may have trouble grasping new information about the Christian life. They may just not understand the process of developing a moral lifestyle.

10. Finally, spiritual autism causes individuals not to focus or explain what they want. A failure to follow directions and a noticeable delay in learning the spiritual language of believers may create more symptoms of a lack of spiritual attention to prayer and the reading of the Word.

Spiritual Attention Deficit (SAD)

It is truly a "sad" day when believers do not listen to good advice and follow mature guidance toward spiritual growth. Understanding a few symptoms of inattention could make one aware of this difficulty. Being a poor listener causes careless mistakes and a failure to follow through on important tasks. Such persons are easily distracted, forgetful in daily activities, and have poor organizational skills. At times, Spiritual Attention Deficit (SAD) causes restlessness with an inability to concentrate on important matters, this may cause one to act on sudden urges that weakens relationships and the ability to influence others in a positive direction.

The big question (or the Elephant in the room) was the person truly converted. Becoming a Christian convert is supposed to drastically change one's life. The easy evangelism of today brings individuals into faith-based groups who have accepted Christ with their mind, but do not have the spiritual and emotional underpinning that brings moral certainty to their life. In other words, their weak conversion experience did not change their life sufficiently to make them a new creation in Christ. It was simply a mental change and not a conversion of the heart. Conversion is similar to the vaccination process where a child receives an injection for immunization against a particular disease. Such an injection normally produces a visible scar and if the mark does not show, the child may need to repeat the process. In other words, "If being born again didn't change your life; try being born again." True conversion brings significant changes in attitude, behavior and lifestyle.

If one remembers the Small Pox vaccinations in school that left a circle scar on the child's arm, they will also recall that some children had to have a second injection. One can only be born again once, but the weak teaching about conversion and weak discipleship causes some to profess the "born again" idea without the spiritual experience. A pastor told the congregation of visiting a dying man and asking if things were right between him and God. The man simply answered "No!" The pastor reminded him that he was baptized as a teenager, but the man responded "Yes, but pastor it didn't take." Then, the pastor whispered, "If the process didn't work, let's repeat the sinner's prayer to make sure." Scripture is clear that one should "examine themselves to see if they are in the faith." Each believer "should make their calling and election sure." Some have said that Christians should not judge others, but I suppose it is OK to be a fruit inspector. "By their fruit shall you know them."

As a child I received instruction both in the Bible and in the Talmud. I am a Jew, but I am enthralled by the luminous figure of the Nazarene. No one can read the Gospels without feeling the actual presence of Jesus. His personality pulsates in every word.
No myth is filled with such life.

— Albert Einstein

CHAPTER SEVEN

Affirming the Destination

Seeing Heaven as the Ultimate Objective

Again, I wish to remind the reader that the destination is worth the journey. When one contemplates the end of life, hopefully, they see Heaven as their ultimate objective. Life is not easy and finding the strength and courage for a lifestyle change is most difficult without the regenerating power of conversion purchased on Calvary by Jesus Himself. Most human beings believe in a Higher Power and worship some form of deity; either the living God or an idol. Many good people populate the earth and some live a good and moral life without the ultimate redemption provided to escape final damnation. When one is openly wicked, they can clearly see the need for redemption. When they know they are lost; they can then seek to be saved. It is often the morally good who do not see the need for conversion.

> 17. Brethren, unite in imitating me and mark those who behave according to my example. 18. (For I have told you before and now tell you again weeping, that many behave as the enemies of the cross of Christ: 19. whose end is punishment in hell, whose stomach is their god, and are proud of their shameful behavior, and are absorbed in

earthly matters.) 20. **For our commonwealth is in heaven; from which place we look for the Savior, the Lord Jesus Christ:** 21. who will change our contemptible body into one fashioned as His glorious body, according to the working of His power whereby He is able to subjugate all things unto Himself. (Philippians 3:12-21 EDNT)

Adverbial Messengers

A believer with a spiritual lifestyle becomes a witness and a kind of adverbial messenger magnifying the spiritual action of others to indicate manner, time, place, cause, or degree and answers questions; such as, how?, when?, where?, why? or to what extent? When an active Christian demonstrates a clear witness, others begin to receive the answers to those questions. How did this salvation come about? When did it happen? Where did it happen? Why are you following the Christian way? To what extent does your message apply to us? Such questions open the door for witnessing about the message of grace.

How did this salvation come about?

Many years ago, God promised a redeeming Messiah, someone who would save the people from trouble or a difficult situation. This Messiah was to be a spiritual leader sent by God to save the world. According to history and religion, Jesus Christ, was that Messiah. He came first to the Jewish people and they rejected Him and cooperated with the Romans to crucify Him. According to Scripture, this Jesus rose from the dead in three days, ascended to heaven, and now sits in authority at the right hand of God, the Father.

Redemption was to come through Israel, but Israel had become a weak nation and had lost political independence to mighty Rome. The weakened faith of Judaism was lost in the despair of the times and Israel was slipping into the evening shadows of hopelessness. Yet the embers of Messianic hope survived for a few and the birth of Jesus was the morning light of a new day for Israel and the world.

8. Meanwhile shepherds nearby were guarding their flock during the night watch. 9. An angel of the Lord stood suddenly by them, and the radiance of divine glory shown round about them: and they were greatly frightened. 10. But the angel commanded, Stop being afraid: for, behold, I announce good news and great joy for all people. 11. Today in the city of David a Deliver is born; who is the Anointed Lord. 12. And this shall be the sign for you; you will find an infant wrapped in linen lying in a manger. 13. And suddenly there appeared the armies of heaven, saying, 14. glory to God on high and peace on earth to men of good-will. 15. When the angels were gone back to heaven, the shepherds said one to another, let us go straight to Bethlehem and see this thing that has happened, which the Lord made known to us. (Luke 2:8-15 EDNT)

When and where did it happen?

Malachi promised that the Sun of righteousness would shine on the people of God. Jesus was to bring light to the darkened world and provide a way for eternal salvation for the human race. Jesus was born in Bethlehem while the world slept in darkness. The singing of a Heavenly Choir that awakened sleepy shepherd to the birth announcement of Jesus was also a wakeup call to a weary world. The message of the Angels caused the shepherds to personally search for and find the Savior (Luke 2:8-18). Wise men followed the Star of Bethlehem and brought gifts to the Christ child. The promised Redeemer received gifts and worship from both shepherds from the hillside and men of wisdom from afar. The shepherds were the first to share the good news of Jesus.

16. And they hurried, and discovered Mary and Joseph, and the child lying in a manger. 17. When they had seen this, they made known abroad all that was told them concerning the child. 18. And all who heard the story of the shepherds were astonished. 19. But Mary guarded these treasured words, and meditated about them in her heart. 20. And the shepherds returned to their flock, glorifying and praising God for all the wonderful things

they had seen and heard, just as they had been told. (Luke 2:16-18 EDNT)

Why are you following the Christian way?

There was a freshness about the life and teachings of Jesus. Even the leaders of Judaism who heard Him said, "Never a man spoke like this man." Jesus went about doing good healing the sick, working miracles, and forgiving sins. Jesus did not claim to be the Messiah, He chose to demonstrate His Deity and to impress upon each individual that He was the Son of God. Jesus said, "The works that I do in My Father's name, they bear witness of Me."

24. Then the Jews encircled Jesus and asked, How long will you leave us in doubt? If you are the Christ, tell us plainly. 25. Jesus answered, I told you, and you did not believe: the works that I do in My Father's name, they bear witness of Me. (John 10:24, 25 EDNT)

Simon Peter established the deity of Jesus when he said, "You are the Christ, the Son of the living God." With this revelation, Jesus could proceed on His divine mission to save the world. Jesus did not hesitate to offer Himself as a sacrifice for the sins of the human race and open the way to redemption for all. With the ransom of the soul, a convert became a new creation with a spiritual lifestyle and the resources to construct a new and better society.

To what extent does your message apply to us? Jesus presented a new discipline to the inner man to change both attitude and behavior. This regeneration created a new predisposition to act in a moral manner. Jesus taught principles rather than specific rules that gave His followers validity and permanency. Through consecrated witnesses, the message of Jesus was to spread around the world. Jesus defined the essential quality of a moral act by teaching the principle of love and the law of right conduct.

25. Teacher, what shall I do to inherit eternal life? 26. He answered, What is written in the text? How do you read it? 27. He answered, You shall love the Lord your God

continually with your whole heart, and with your whole soul, and with your whole strength, and with your whole mind; and your neighbor as yourself. 28. Jesus said, That is correct: do this and you shall live. (Luke 10:25-28 EDNT)

The message of salvation is open to all who will believe and behave the teachings of Jesus. Salvation is not "fire insurance" to escape eternal punishment; it is open to those who are ready and willing to change their lifestyle and live a life of moral witness. Salvation separates one from personal sins not their family and friends. Once an individual receives salvation, they develop an aggressive willingness to share the good news of the gospel to both friend and foe. The transformation that takes place in the conversion process is so absolute that the convert is enabled to follow the demands of Jesus.

Jesus taught a righteousness that exceeded the Law of Moses. The righteousness was to spring out of love and produce respect for others. Jesus insisted on more respect for women as an equal partner in life and grace. He required that one respect the personal reputation of everyone and demanded initiative in friendship. Jesus stipulated true motives in worship that included faith in the future. This required honest dealings with others and required being a faithful witness to the grace of Jesus. A dynamic and growing spiritual experience transforms individuals with a desire to share the good news of salvation with others.

Ambassadors with a Message

Ambassadors are emissaries carrying messages to others. Followers who believed became converts, then disciples (learners), and ultimately special messengers (or apostles). Apostles are more than messengers they are companions and proponents supporting a cause or a person. They are proponents because they argue in favor of both the message and the sender of the message. Believers who follow Jesus become true supporters who both carry His message and internalize the value of the message. They are change agents accepting personal change in the process of changing others. These true spiritual ambassadors have a lifestyle of witness to all who will observe their behavior or listen to their testimony. Personal witness is the means by which believers disseminate the moral and redeeming message. For example, after a personal conversion experience, Paul told King Agrippa:

> I did not disobey the heavenly vision: 20. but first I told the inhabitants of Damascus and Jerusalem, and then the rest of Judea and finally to the Gentiles, **that they should repent and turn to God, and live a life consistent with that change of heart** (Acts 26:19-20 EDNT).

Almost Disciples

Some are close to repentance and near to salvation but become "almost disciples." They permit some barrier to come between them and promise of eternal life. The world is full of good individuals who live honest and decent lives, but have never made a faith-based commitment to an empowered life in Christ. Such are individuals who follow at a distance and never move close enough to develop a lifestyle influenced by the teachings of Jesus. Luke's Gospel describes three such almost disciples (Luke 9:57-62). **The first example was one who wanted to follow Jesus without understanding the meaning of true discipleship.** A follower of Jesus is called from a life of ease to one of self-sacrifice and service. Today the message of grace must come from committed learners who shine the light of grace on the lives of others. Their faith-based behavior attracts individuals to become involved with the Christian experience. A fascination with developing a faith-based lifestyle can enable a true follower of Jesus and be assured of entrance into the Heavenly City.

Barrier of Custom

The second almost disciple was called to follow Jesus, but this person wanted to bury his father first. In fact, according to Moses, this was not an immediate responsibility but he wanted to follow the custom of waiting until his father's death to plan the rest of his life. **This was an unreasonable delay to the call of Jesus.** When the opportunity came, it was critical that he make an immediate choice to follow Jesus. Not even custom or the Law, may become a barrier to a faith-based lifestyle. Those attracted to Jesus must follow His rules and guidelines without hesitation. These are the term of true faith-based discipleship.

Unwilling to give priority

The third almost disciple wanted to stipulate the terms and conditions under which he would follow Jesus. Unwilling to give priority to the call of Jesus, he permitted his family and friends to become a barrier between Christ and himself. Family and friends are important, but must not be the reason one fails to follow Jesus, the source of Eternal Life. As hard as it seems, Christ demands first place in the commitment of His followers. **This almost disciple wanted to follow Jesus but insisted on his own terms: his time, his place, his price.** This attitude could never produce a true disciple or a lifestyle of faith-based behavior. These three examples from Luke illustrate the basic difficulties of hearing the call of Christ, forsaking all, denying self, counting the cost of discipleship, and following Christ with total commitment. There is no easy discipleship. Yet the price of a spiritual life on earth and Eternal Life is a true bargain. Why would one refuse to accept such a good deal?

One thing you Lack

Scripture records an incident where a wealthy young man wanted to follow Jesus, but was unwilling to commit to assisting the poor. **This one thing caused the young man, who had followed the Ten Commandments from his youth, to become grief-stricken and fail to follow Jesus.** [An unwritten action here is clear: "And Jesus let him go!"] To develop a faith-based lifestyle that produces moral behavior requires complete commitment to the rules and guidelines of Jesus.

One Thing You Lack

18. A man of the ruling class asked Jesus, saying, Good Teacher, what shall I do to inherit eternal life? 19. And Jesus answered, Why do you call Me good? No one is good, save God. 20. You know the commandments, Do not be unfaithful in marriage, Do not murder, Do not take what is not yours, Do not say anything false about others, Honor your father and your mother. 21. And he said, All these I have kept from my youth. 22. When Jesus heard this, He said, **Yet one thing you lack: sell all your possessions, and distribute it among the poor, and you will have treasure in heaven: then return and follow me.** 23. And when he heard this, he was distressed: for he was a wealthy man. 24. When Jesus saw he was grief-stricken, He said, With great difficulty shall the wealthy enter the kingdom of God! 25. For it may be easier for a camel to squeeze through a surgical needle's eye, than for a wealthy man to enter the kingdom of God. 26. **And those who heard this asked, Who then can be saved? 27. And Jesus said, The things that are impossible with men are possible with God.** 28. And Peter said, We have left all and followed you. 29. And Jesus said, Truly, I say, Those who left home, parents, brothers, wife, or children, for sake of the kingdom of God, 30. **will receive in this present time much more and in the world to come everlasting life.** (Luke 18:18-30 EDNT)

Almost was not enough

When Paul appeared before King Agrippa, a Jew, Paul was accused by Festus of being a fanatic, but he witnessed with straight truth and seriousness. Because Agrippa believed in the Prophets and was influenced by Paul's witness, Agrippa said, **"Almost you persuade me to become a Christian."** Almost was not enough. Total commitment to Christ is required to live a faith-based life.

25. But Paul said, I am not fanatical, most noble Festus: but **I speak nothing but straight truth with seriousness. 26. And King Agrippa is aware of these matters and I can speak freely before him: for I am convinced that**

all this is common knowledge to him; for these things were not done in some secret corner. 27. King Agrippa, Do you believe the prophets? I know that you believe. 28. Then Agrippa said to Paul, **Almost you persuade me to become a Christian.** 29. And Paul said, I pray to God that not only you, but also all who hear me this day, were both almost and altogether as I am, except these chains. (Acts 26:25-29 EDNT)

Faith without Works is Void

Many in the past have seen the value of the actual presence of Jesus without ever trusting Him for salvation. An honest faith or mental knowledge about the historical Jesus is not sufficient to produce eternal life for the soul. There must be more than intellectual apprehension of facts. There must be acceptance of Jesus, the Way, the Truth, and the Life, in a personal act of faith. To read and believe the facts of the New Testament alone will never bring redemption to the heart and soul of man. An example of exposure to the Gospels without taking the personal step of faith is clear in the words of Einstein:

> As a child I received instruction both in the Bible and in the Talmud. I am a Jew, but I am enthralled by the luminous figure of the Nazarene. No one can read the Gospels without feeling the actual presence of Jesus. His personality pulsates in every word. No myth is filled with such life. (Albert Einstein wrote in the Saturday Evening Post October 26, 1926.)

Thanks To God

> 14. Now, thanks to God who always causes us to triumph in Christ, and makes us the sweet fragrance of his knowledge in every place. 15. For we are the sweet incense of Christ offered to God, that makes manifest those being saved and those who are perishing: 16. to the one we are the odor of death that precedes the grave; and to the other the fragrance of life that promises life eternal. (2 Corinthians 2:14-16 EDNT)

My daddy would say to me

*"I don't want to know the storms that you encounter.
Just bring the ship ashore."*

— Dipnarine Ramjattan

CHAPTER EIGHT

Sailing through the Storms

The beautiful and noble ship with all her precious wealth
speeds away gaily and safe.
But O the ship, the immortal ship! O ship aboard the ship!
Ship of the body, ship of the soul, voyaging, voyaging,..

From "Aboard at a Ship's Helm"

— Walt Whitman

When the pressure of adversity comes and the winds of sorrow blow, just do like the eagle that puts out his wings during the storm and just keeps circling and lets the pressure lift him above the storm. Say "yes" to God and "no" to the circumstances. You can overcome; you can have a faith that prevails. The words to the chorus express this positive affirmation:

Yes, Lord, yes, to your will and to your way.
Yes, Lord, yes, I will trust you and obey.
When your Spirit speaks to me,
With my whole heart I'll agree,
And my answer will be yes, Lord, yes.

— Lynn Keesecker

The Lord will never fail His children. Alone they may fumble and fail, but with trust in God, they will overcome. Act on faith and take charge of the circumstance. Nothing will happen today that you and God together cannot handle. You cannot only sail through the storm but with faith, you can navigate through any difficulty the human condition throws at you. One young man when encouraged to fly above the storm asked, "How can I fly with the eagles when I have to work every day with turkeys?" God has a plan to assist believers over the fence, up the hill, across the river, and through the valley, if they will only follow His lead.

With conversion comes lifestyle changes that are the initial evidence that one has been born again. "Therefore if any man be in Christ, he is **a new creation: observe, the old things have passed away; all things have become new."** (2 Corinthians 5:17 EDNT) If an individual is troubled about a moral lifestyle, the following lifestyle changes may improve their walk with Christ.

Ship Ahoy

— M. J. Cartwright (1889)

I was drifting away on life's pitiless sea,
And the angry waves threatened my ruin to be,
When away at my side, there I dimly descried,
A stately old vessel, and loudly I cried:
"Ship ahoy! Ship ahoy!"
And loudly I cried: "Ship ahoy!"

'Twas the "old ship of Zion," thus sailing along,
All aboard her seemed joyous, I heard their sweet song;
And the Captain's kind ear, ever ready to hear,
Caught my wail of distress, as I cried out in fear:
"Ship ahoy! Ship ahoy!"
As I cried out in fear: "Ship ahoy!"

The good Captain commanded a boat to be low'red,
And with tender compassion He took me on board;
And I'm happy today, all my sins washed away
In the blood of my Savior, and now I can say:
"Bless the Lord! Bless the Lord!"
From my soul I can say: "Bless the Lord!"

O soul, sinking down 'neath sin's merciless wave,
The strong arm of our Captain is mighty to save;
Then trust Him today, no longer delay,
Board the old ship of Zion, and shout on your way:
"Jesus saves! Jesus saves!"
Shout and sing on your way: "Jesus saves!"

Start daily with the Lord: scripture is clear that believers must walk by faith and keep their eyes on Jesus. Just 30 minutes of daily walking with the Lord in the devotional reading of the New Testament will work wonders for your spiritual health. This reading should primarily be in the New Testament. This is because this portion of scripture is the new covenant after the Crucifixion of Christ. The New Testament contains the guidelines for traveling the Right Path. The Old Testament was a "schoolmaster to bring us to Christ" now believer must follow the guidelines clearly expressed in the New Covenant. A prayerful approach to reading the words of the New Testament can strengthen your present walk with Christ.

> 22. But in scripture the Law makes all men guilty, that the promise by faith in Jesus Christ might be given to them who believe. 23. But before faith came, we were shut up in bondage to the law, until faith was afterwards revealed. 24. Wherefore the law was a truant officer to keep us in school and a teacher's aide to guide our learning until the True Teacher, Christ, came that we might learn justification by faith. 25. But after faith came, we no longer needed a truant officer or a teacher's aide. 26. For we are all the children of God by faith in Christ Jesus. 27. For as many as have been identified with Christ by baptism have been clothed with the attributes of Christ. 28. In Christ there is

neither Jew nor Greek, bond nor free, male or female; for you are all one in Christ Jesus. (Galatians 3:22-28 EDNT)

Consume the proper food from the Word: the New Testament contains the milk of the word, the fruit of the Spirit and the meat of the Gospel.

1. You must put aside all insincerity, jealous feelings, and all back-biting, 2. **Since you are newly born, yearn for the unadulterated milk of the word, so you may grow up until your soul thrives in good health. 3. Since you have tasked the Lord's kindness. 4. Draw near to him;** (1 Peter 2:1-3 EDNT)

11. The story laid upon me is long and hard to explain, seeing you are so dull of hearing. 12. After all this time you should be teachers, yet you still need to be taught again the first principles of the divine revelation: you have gone back to needing milk instead of solid food. 13. **Those who still have milk for their diet does not have the experience to speak of what is right: remains an infant. 14. But grown men can eat solid food, those who, through the development of the right kind of habit, have reached a stage when their perceptions are trained to distinguish between good and evil.** (Hebrews 5:11-14 EDNT)

Beware of Religious Junk Food

There are many substitutes for the real thing. Some suggest that Coca Cola is the "real thing," but in the realm of religion Jesus is "the Way, the Truth, and the Life." Without even looking for reading material, new, young, or weak Christians will encounter much material that was prepared for profit and marketed to promote a personality. Be careful what you read or listen to on TV, a CD, tape, or the Internet.

It is best to spend most of your spiritual development reading in the New Testament. Yes, the Old Testament has many good stories, but the New Testament is the "true message" prepared and preserved for believers. Be careful that you do not spend your Bible reading time rummaging through the old stories of Jewish or pre-Christian history. All the rules and guidance for a moral Christian lifestyle are in the New Testament. God preserved this new covenant for believers. To become a strong witness with a moral lifestyle read, believe and behave the words recorded in the New Testament.

Choose the books and authors you read carefully and be certain that most of your reading time is actually in the New Testament. The goal is to please both God and reach others with the true message of grace. Religious "junk food" may taste good, but the spiritual nutritional benefits are questionable.

Diet of Kings, Princes, and Paupers

There is an old saying relative to the way one should eat to stay healthy. The suggestion was to eat properly but in diminishing amounts. Eat a big meal in the morning, a less but well proportioned meal at noon, and a small meal in the evening. A King would eat large meals to establish and maintain stamina to carry him through a busy day of kingdom work. While a Prince would eat well but less than the king, and contemplate his future place in kingdom. While an impoverished man, such as a Pauper, would eat what was available with thanksgiving.

Applying dietary portions to a believer's regular prayer and devotional reading includes a menu of prayer, the milk of the Word, the fruit of the Spirit, and the meat of the Gospel. These options are proper spiritual nourishment for believers, and can become comfort food for the Calvary road when the daily portions are adequate and properly consumed.

When a believer prays as a King would in the morning and as a Prince would at lunchtime and then as a Pauper would in the evening, well-equipped believers with spiritual health would be equal to their daily task. In this application, imagine how a believer would daily apply the process to their daily devotional life. Perhaps a King would pray for his kingdom and all the people that they would live in peace and prosperity. A Prince would probably look to the future when he would rule in the kingdom and pray to be prepared and equal to the task. And a Pauper who must depend on others for food, shelter, and other essentials, would eat what was available and proceed with hope in his heart that things would be better tomorrow.

Kingly portions of a spiritual diet are important to provide stamina for a devout and productive life in the kingdom. A King would have access to the best nourishment available, and so should each believer. A Prince, not yet fully vested in kingdom responsibilities, would have a healthy died as he developed into a trusted and productive member of kingdom. A Pauper, with limited opportunities for food and nourishment, would take advantage of each opportunity to obtain food to strengthen their daily life. A view of the prayer that Jesus taught His disciples and the special portion applied to king, prince, pauper, and all:

THE LORD'S PRAYER

KING
Our Father who art in heaven, hallowed be Thy name,
Thy kingdom come,

PRINCE
Thy will be done, on earth as it is in heaven,

PAUPER
Give us this day our daily bread and forgive us our trespasses as we
forgive those who trespass against us and lead us not into temptation,
but deliver us from evil.

ALL
For Thine is the kingdom and the power and the glory
Now and forever, Amen!

Check your Heart and Vascular Health

Vascular health in the human anatomy relates to the blood carrying vessels. This system is the human network to supply life to the physical body through the arteries, veins, and capillaries to and from the heart. In this supply system, any problems can be serious. Arteries can become thick and stiff. Clots can clog the vessels and block blood flow to the heart and brain. Weakened vessels can burst, causing internal bleeding. The older one becomes the more likely to have vascular disease. Long periods of sitting or standing still can complicate the flow of blood and cause disease of the heart. Scripture is clear about the flow of blood in the body as the source of life. "The life of the body is in the blood" (Leviticus 17:11 DOT). A recorded proverb "A sound heart is the life of the body: but greed and envious desire are the decay of the body." (Proverbs 14:30 DOT) Both physical and spiritual health depends on the flow of blood; this includes the redemptive flow of the blood of Jesus that brings spiritual wholeness to the believer.

Watch your intake of Sweets

The word "sweet" at times is a substitute for such words as: appealing, attractive, adorable, lovable, charming, delightful, pleasing to the senses, satisfying and softhearted. It appears that many of these synonyms clearly express the assets and benefits of consistent personal prayer. The life and ministry of a blind English preacher, W. W. Walford, would combine all these and other synonyms into lyrics about prayer. Walford was a man of obscure birth and no education, but a praying man of strong mind with a great memory. In the pulpit, he quoted the scripture lesson with precision giving chapter and verse. He was certain that there were no substitutes for the sweetness of personal prayer. At times, he attempted poetry. One such poem expressed the value of prayer and became the lyrics of the hymn Sweet Hour of Prayer:

> *Sweet hour of prayer! Sweet hour of prayer!*
> *That calls me from a world of care,*
> *And bids me at my Father's throne*
> *Make all my wants and wishes known.*

In seasons of distress and grief,
My soul has often found relief
And oft escaped the tempter's snare
By thy return, sweet hour of prayer!

— William W. Walford (1845)

Exercise all your Muscles

The overcoming attitude is one that perseveres. Coaches and trainers in sports are able to develop such an attitude with athletes. A runner may be told, "If you don't win, the fellow who beats you better break a record." Never give up and never quit are clear guidance to athletes. Young players stay in the game with injuries that should hospitalize them, but their will to persevere and their determination is so strong they continue. Should there be any less resolve and perseverance among the followers of Jesus? Must the Kingdom of Christ be plagued with weary or discouraged followers? Scripture provides guidance for the spiritual race:

Practice rigid self-control

25. And every man **who enters the race practices rigid self-control. They do this to win a wreath that will soon wither, but we seek a crown that will not fade.** 26. I run but not aimlessly; so I fight, but not as a shadow boxer: 27. But I beat my body black and blue, and bring it into subjection: lest by any means, when I have preached to others, I myself should be rejected as a worthless coin. (1 Corinthians 9:25-27 EDNT)

Two sets of Muscles

Scripture suggests that healthy believers can run and not grow weary, walk and not faint. This is spiritual physical fitness. The big question is "Have you developed this capacity? Have you exercised and developed all your muscles? Are you willing to persevere until all your private limitations are over come? Remember, the heart is a muscle."

In the military, young men learn this lesson in a most difficult manner. Just a few days before they could not make a bed, carry out the garbage, mow the lawn, pick up their clothes, or wash behind their ears without their mother standing over them. Suddenly, these same young men are clean shaven, able to make a bed that bounces a coin, glad to march all day and even able to make a twenty-five (25) mile hike carrying a weapon and full gear. What was the change? It was the development of discipline and a winning attitude. It was the awareness that they were part of a team. Knowing that others depended on them kept them going. They developed this confident attitude partially because their military trainers understood that they had walking muscles and running muscles. Can Christian leaders not spiritually train new converts to persevere?

On a long march, a Sergeant walks along with the troops until they become leg weary, then he orders, "Double time, March!" Now they must go twice as fast as before. It would never be appropriate to stop; they must try to follow orders. Surprisingly, their legs seemed rested and worked well as they marched at double time pace (180 steps a minute). Even though they were about to fall at the slower pace, now they felt refreshed and ready for the race. What was the difference?

Humans have two sets of muscles: walking muscles and running muscles. While they were marching, their running muscles were at rest. Now, at the double time speed, their walking muscles were resting. About the time the running muscles were getting fatigued, the mean old Sergeant, gives an order to return to the regular march cadence. Again, the young men are surprised that they can continue. They actually feel refreshed. Their confidence grows. They now realize how young and strong they are and are ready to follow orders and face all enemies. Spiritual discipline can create the same attitude and staying power for the spiritual race.

Self-discipline and a short rest at the halfway mark had prepared them for the Sergeant's order: "It's just 12 miles to camp. If we hurry we can make chow!" They are hungry and ready. By the time they reach camp, they are a fighting team with an overcoming attitude. Proper leadership and self-discipline made the difference.

Run and not be weary walk and not faint.

30. Even the youths shall faint and be weary, and the young men shall utterly fall: 31. But they that wait upon the Lord shall renew their strength; they shall mount up with wings as eagles, **they shall run, and not be weary; and they shall walk, and not faint.** (Isaiah 40:30 - 31)

You were running the race well; who cut in to obstruct your obedience of the truth? (Galatians 5:7 EDNT)

Self-discipline

11. The time is now that you must awake to reality: for salvation is nearer that when we first believed. 12. The night is almost over and dawn is near: let us therefore lay aside the clothing of the night, and put on the weapons of light. 13. Let us behave honestly in the day light; not in partying and intoxicated behavior, not in secret places of immorality, not in conflict and greed. 14. But clothe yourselves with the Lord Jesus Christ, and make no plans to fulfill the desires of the flesh. (Romans 13:11-14 EDNT)

Who would believe it?

This is a true story about a Texas Liquor Business wanting to expand their building and a local church through petitions and prayers tried to stop the growth of liquor sales. About a week before the expansion was complete and before the grand re-opening, a bolt of lightning struck the bar and burned it to the ground. The church members were excited and bragged about "the power of prayer." The owner of the bar was so angry that he eventually sued the church on grounds that they "were ultimately responsible for the destruction of his building, through direct actions or indirect means." Lawyers for the church denied all responsibility or any connection to the building's destruction.

The judge read carefully through the plaintiff's complaint and the defendant's reply. He then opened the hearing by saying: "I don't know how I'm going to decide this case, but for now it appears from the paperwork that what we have here is a bar owner who now believes in the power of prayer, and an entire church congregation that claims their prayers did not cause the lightning or the fire."

A Dog and a Purse

There is a story coming out of the middle ages about a dog bringing funds to a hungry man. It is different from the scriptural account of Peter finding coins in the mouth of a fish to pay taxes for Jesus and himself. It is true that where God guides, He provides. Why is this lesson so hard to learn?

A Scottish man named John Craig, studied at the University of St. Andrews, and entered the ministry. From reading Calvin's works, John became a Protestant resulting in his arrest and being taken prisoner to Rome where he was condemned to death. While waiting execution, the Pope died and according to Roman custom, the doors of all prisons were to open. The escape of John Craig was facilitated by this custom, but he was soon tracked down and captured by soldiers. Among the soldiers was a previously wounded soldier whom John Craig had assisted. Because it was within his power, this soldier released John, gave him money, and mapped out a safe route for him to travel toward his home.

Soon the money and the food were exhausted and in despair, John lay down in the woods to rest and consider his options. Hearing a noise, he was fearful, but it was only a dog. In the dog's mouth was a purse, the dog came close and left the purse near the desperate man. With the funds in the purse, John traveled and received further assistance to reach his home in Scotland by some who heard his testimony. There he preached Christ and witnessed of God's power until his death at age eighty-eight. God works wonders to enable His followers to live a moral lifestyle that witnesses to His power.

God makes provision for His children; David (Psalm 37:25) wrote that he had never seen the righteous forsaken, nor God's seed begging bread. Scripture is clear, God does not forsake his own. They may be tested and tried, but that is part of God's plan to strengthen their character and improve their moral lifestyle. St. Paul expressed it this way:

> 8. We are pressed on every side, yet not hemmed in, we are bewildered, but never at a loss; 9. persecuted, but not abandoned; knocked down, but never counted out; (2 Corithians 4: 8-9 EDNT)

An Aggressive Lifestyle

John Foxe, an Oxford trained minister in Elizabethan England, became troubled by the news of Christian leaders being captured and burned at the stake. The idea of reporting this persecution soon obsessed him and he began a life-long effort to record a history of individuals who gave their lives because of their stand and protest against those who were persecuting believers who embraced the protestant idea. Foxe lived on the edge of poverty, worked in a print shop to support his family and labored late in the evening researching and writing about Christian martyrs. Over many years, he developed a manuscript over two thousand pages documenting the records of martyrs who witnessed to the Christian faith with the sacrifice of their lives. We now know his work as the Foxe's Book of Martyrs, the crowning achievement of his work written by flickering candlelight. This effort took a toll on his physical health and Foxe died of weariness, but the world now has a great cloud of witnesses that speak to an aggressive lifestyle of moral witness. Paul understood the process and recorded his personal testimony:

16. The Holy Spirit joins with our human spirit confirming that we are the children of God: 17. since we are children, then heirs, and fellow heirs with Christ; if we suffer together we may also be glorified together. 18. **For I consider the sufferings we now endure not worthy to be compared with the glory about to be revealed in us** (Romans 8:16-18 EDNT).

Burdens and Blessings

John Fawcett pastored a poor Baptist church in England, but found time to write. The news of his writing spread and the largest church in England called him as pastor. With everything packed to move, John's wife wanted to understand if they were doing the right thing? "Will we ever find people who love us as these folk do?" John agreed and they decided to stay for the rest of their life in the small church. Out of this experience, John Fawcett wrote the world-famous hymn:

> *Blest be the tie that binds*
> *Our hearts in Christian love,*
> *The fellowship of kindred minds*
> *Is like to that above.*

There is a need for fellowship that exceeds fame and fortune. To do the work of God among and with the support of true friends has a spiritual value that no material gain can match. Those of us who have support from a spouse, family members and friends are indeed fortunate. This privilege enhances the blessings of the moral lifestyle and opens many doors for witnessing and sharing the truths of the Word. Praise to God and those who follow Jesus!

The Christian way is for each man to carry his own load; however, there are times when others must share in the burden bearing. Paul in the same chapter of Galatians (6) tells believers to bear one another's burdens also declared that each one should bear up under his own burden.

Obviously, there are personal concerns that must remain private, but also there are loads that are too heavy for one individual. An example would be a military troop on the move.

Each soldier must carry his own weapon and supplies, but the equipment of the mess tent and other heavy battle gear for the benefit of all, needs more than one to move the equipment for the group. The unwillingness of others to assist in carrying the group load may be one reason for so much strife and discontent in organized religion. Two or three may validate a witness and establish cooperation among the group. Community outreach and soul winning are shared group responsibilities. Without the confirmation of a committed group of practicing believers, the individual testimony has little value to one on the outside. The knowledge of a loving and believing community is a strong foundation for personal witnessing of God's redemptive plan.

When a new convert was asking God for almost everything from fixing the roof to repairs of the restroom facilities, an older Christian said, "Don't bother God with those things that you can fix yourself!" The new convert's answer was revealing, "I am a new Christian excited about serving a big God and it doesn't lessen God a bit to do little things for me. Someday I will be an old Christian and just bear burdens like you." There is tragic truth in this situation. Mature believes must permit new converts to enjoy the greatness of God and give them time to grow in grace and knowledge. I hope that they will become joyful burden bearers and take pleasure in assisting others with their load.

The Second Mile

The lesson of the "second mile" is a good one to learn (Matthew 5:41). A Roman soldier could compel a stranger to carry his load for one mile, but no more. Jesus told his followers, "If one compels you to carry his load one mile, carry the load two." The first mile is out of duty; the second is for love. The first mile may serve a purpose as an act of obedience, but the second mile becomes a witness and an open door for discussion as to the character of the load-carrier and the attitude toward the task. I am confident that many who were singled out to carry a Roman soldier's load, must at first resented the task. When the words of Jesus were remembered and the decision made to go the second mile, the whole of the attitude and the environment changed for the better. Obedient discipline has its own reward.

> 11. At the time all discipline is painful rather than pleasant; but afterwards, when it has done the work of discipline, it yields a harvest of good fruit in a righteous life for those trained by the experience. (Hebrews 12:11 EDNT)

Would it not be wonderful if believers constantly expressed the attitude, "Here, let me help you with that burden!" When tragedy or major trouble hits a community, many ask "Why me, Lord?" In reality, a mature believer should ask "Why, not me?" This may sound unreasonable, but believers are to prefer that benefits abound to their friends. In fact, mature believers are to even love their enemies and pray for others who are spiteful toward them. This is a mark of maturity.

All believers are on the same ship going toward the same peaceful harbor of Heaven. The journey is a common venture with all hands on deck and working together. This means each one must do their assigned tasks and join in the work and worship that are part of the same ship. Believers must rejoice and with the eyes of faith see the end of the journey that God has prepared for those who love Him. The full surrendered life is a great joy. Obedience brings joy to the soul and becomes a living witness to others along the way.

Lord, take my life, and make it wholly Thine;
Fill my poor heart with Thy great love divine;
Take all my will, my passion, self, and pride;
I now surrender, Lord — in me abide!

— J. Edwin Orr

CHAPTER NINE

Seeing the Harbor Lights

Oh, I can almost see the lights of that city;
I see them gathering all around the great wide throne.
Through faith in my savior and His wonderful love.
Oh, I can almost see the lights of home.

— Belinda Johnson

Boarding the Ship of Zion is not for a leisure voyage, a lover's sunset ride, or a dinner cruise with friends; it is a long distance passenger ship from earth to heaven. There are no ports of call along the way and no overnight or day excursions to see the sights. The seas of life may be contrary, but this ship is on a serious journey that requires commitment and confidence in the crew and the ship. It is a long journey and one cannot always see the lights of the harbor. It is not always smooth sailing. There are storms, contrary winds, strong currents, fog and rain, but the ship has a steady Captain. With friends and family aboard, and Jesus at the Helm, we are assured of safe passage until we reach the safe harbor on the eternal shores. There will be great rejoicing when we see the lights of the harbor.

Comparison: Guards of the Tomb and Soldiers of the Cross

At the Tomb of the Unknown Soldier, the United States honors their war dead who could not be identified. This information is relevant to the concept of this book, Navigation the Challenges of Faith-based Behavior. It is altogether proper to honor those who gave their life in defense of others; it is even a greater tribute to the loss when those who were unidentifiable because of the nature of their wounds. When comparing the process of honoring unknown fallen warriors with the practice of honoring the life, death and resurrection of Jesus Christ, surely the rules and guidance for those who follow Christ are reasonable and logical. Observe closely the regulations for the Honor Guards of the Tomb at Arlington National Cemetery and how the behavior of the guards compare with the lifestyle of born again believers. [Relevant scriptures noted and numbered for comparison; follow the numbers (1-7) to the verses below]

Especially selected soldiers have continuously guarded The Tomb of the Unknown Soldier day and night, since 1930. The military has rules for those who guard the Tomb; such as, the number of steps taken during the walk past the tomb. The number of steps refers to the twenty-one gun salute the highest honor given any military or foreign dignitary. For the same reason, the guard is required to hesitate for 21 seconds after his about face to begin the return walk. The guard's gloves must be moistened to prevent losing grip on his rifle. The guard is to carry the rifle on the shoulder away from the tomb so when he returns his walk, the rifle is on the opposite shoulder. (Ephesians 6: 10-20) **[1]**

[1] The complete Armor

> 10. Finally, my brothers, be strengthened in the Lord, and in the power of His unlimited resource. 11. **Wear the complete armor of God**, so you can stand against the strategy and assault of the adversary. 12. For our wrestling is not against a physical enemy, but against evil princes

of darkness who rule this world, against hosts of spiritual wickedness in heavenly warfare. 13. Wherefore wear the complete armor of God that you may be able to withstand evil attacks when they come, and be found still standing. 14. Stand your ground, being protected by truth, and having integrity for a breastplate; 15. and the gospel of peace preparing your feet for battle, 16. Above all, take the shield of faith to extinguish all the fiery darts of the wicked. 17. And take the helmet which is salvation, and the sword of the Spirit, which is the word of God: 18. Praying on every occasion through petition in the Spirit, and vigilant with unwearied perseverance and supplication for all saints; (Ephesians 6: 10-19 EDNT).

The guards at the Tomb change every thirty minutes, 24 hours a day, 365 days a year. The guards selected for this service must apply for the duty and be between 5'10" and 6'2" tall with a waist size that does not exceed 30 inches. They must commit two years of active service to guard the tomb and live in barracks under the tomb and cannot drink alcohol on or off duty for the rest of their lives. They cannot swear in public for the rest of their lives and cannot disgrace the uniform or the tomb in any way. (1 Thessalonians 5: 5-11) **[2]**

[2] Be Watchful and Sober

5. Brothers you are not in the dark because you are the children of light, and the children of the day. 6. We must not sleep as others do, but let us be watchful and sober. 7. Night is the time for sleeping and the drunkard's time for drinking. 8. We must remain sober as men of the daylight. We must put on the breastplate of faith and love, the helmet, which is the hope of salvation. 9. God has not destined us for vengeance; He means us to gain salvation through our Lord Jesus Christ, 10. Who died for us, that, whether we wake or sleep, we should live together with Him. 11. Go on encouraging one another and building up one another's faith, as you have been doing. (1 Thessalonians 5:5-11 EDNT).

[2] Habitually Behave in Love

1. Become imitators of God, as His beloved children; 2. and **habitually behave in love**, as Christ loved you, and was delivered for you as an offering and voluntary sacrifice to God to become a pleasing fragrance. 3. But as saints let not immorality, impurity or callous greediness, be named even once among you; 4. neither obscenity, nor corrupt talking, nor practiced suggestive speech, these are all unbecoming behavior: but rather give thanks. 5. For this you surely know, that no solicitor for prostitutes, or reckless spendthrift, or worshiper of idols, will have a place in the kingdom of Christ and of God. 6. Let no man mislead you with words devoid of truth: because these things bring the anger of God upon the disobedient. 7. Do not associate with such things. 8. For once your heart was in darkness, but now it is filled with light from the Lord: behave as the product of light: 9. (for the product of light is seen in all goodness, righteousness, and sincerity;) 10. be living proof of what is well-pleasing to the Lord. 11. And have no friendship with the activities of darkness, but rather admonish them. (Ephesians 5:1-11 EDNT)

Every guard spends five hours a day getting his uniform ready for duty. He wears specially made shoes with extra thick soles to keep the heat and cold from their feet. They have metal heel plates that extend to the top of the shoe in order to make the loud click as they come to a halt. There must be no wrinkles, folds or lint on their uniform. Guards dress for duty in front of a full-length mirror. (1 Corinthians 13:12-13) **[3]**

[3] Seeing Yourself in a Mirror

12. At the present we see only blurred reflections in polished metal; but then face to face the blurred image will be gone and we will see ourselves as God sees us. 13. Now there are three things that endure forever faith, hope, and love; but the greatest of these is love. (1 Corinthians 13: 12-13 EDNT)

[3] Without Spot or Wrinkle

11. It is for you, servant of God, to run from these things; and pursue righteousness, godliness, faith, love, endurance, and be teachable. 12. Struggle to win the good fight of faith and grasp eternal life, to which you were called, now that you have witnesses to your noble profession. 13. I charge before God, the one making all things live and Christ Jesus the one having witnessed the good confession in the time of Pontius Pilate. 14. **That you execute your charge without spot or blame**, until our Lord Jesus Christ appears: (1 Timothy 6:11-14 EDNT)

During the first six months of duty, a guard cannot talk to anyone or watch TV. They spend all off duty time studying the 175 notable individuals laid to rest in Arlington National Cemetery. A guard must memorize who they are and be able to locate their grave. After two years of service, the guard is given a wreath pin (James 1:12) **[4]** that is worn on their lapel signifying they served as a guard of the tomb. There are only 400 presently worn. The guard must obey these rules for the rest of their lives or give up the wreath pin. (2 Timothy 1:3-9; 2 Timothy 2:15-16) **[5]**

[4] A Badge of Honor

12. Blood related and fortunate is the man who flinches not under the enticement of testing: for when he is proved trustworthy, he shall be given the **wreath of honor** that verifies vitality, which God promised to all who worship out of a benevolent heart. (James 1:12 EDNT)

[5] A Workman Unashamed

15. Be eager to present yourself approved to God, **a workman unashamed, cutting straight the word of truth**. 16. But avoid blasphemous and worthless chatter: for they will cause more disobeying of the word. (2 Timothy 2: 15-16 EDNT)

[5] Share Hardships as a Soldier

> 3. **Join the ranks of those who share hardships as a soldier** of Jesus Christ. 4. No active warrior entangles himself with ordinary affairs; so he may please the one who enlisted him as a soldier. 5. And also if anyone wrestles, **he is not crowned unless he wrestles lawfully.** 6. The hardworking farmer must be the first to partake of the fruits. 7. Consider what I say; for the Lord will give you understanding in all things. 8. Keep remembering that Jesus Christ, a descendent of David was raised from the dead and was the theme of my gospel: 9. This gospel for which I suffer, even in chains as an evil doer, but the word of God is not bound (2 Timothy 1:3-9 EDNT).

When Hurricane Isabelle was approaching Washington, DC, the US Senate and House took two days off with anticipation of the storm. Because of the dangers from the hurricane, the guards assigned to the Tomb of the Unknown Soldier had permission to suspend their assignment. They respectfully declined saying, "No way, Sir!" Soaked to the skin, marching in the pelting rain of a tropical storm, they said that guarding the Tomb was not just an assignment; it was the highest honor assignment available to a serviceperson. (1 Timothy 6: 20-21; 2 Timothy 1: 13-14) **[6]**

[6] Keep Safe what has been entrusted to you

> 20. Timothy, **keep safe what has been entrusted to you,** avoiding profane and frivolous talk, and the contradictions of false knowledge: 21. Some have missed the mark professing false knowledge concerning the faith. (1 Timothy 6: 20-21 EDNT)

[6] Guard the Trust

> 13. Retain the standard of healthy words in faith and love in Christ Jesus, which you heard from me. 14. **Guard the trust that was committed to you** by the Holy Spirit which dwells in us. (2 Timothy 1:13-14 EDNT)

Christians can clearly identify the One who gave His life for the salvation of others. When compared with the facts of the death and resurrection of the author of eternal salvation, it is reasonable to have rules and specific guidance for those who honor His life. (2 Timothy 1:12) **[7]**

[7] I Know

12. For which cause, I also suffer these things: nevertheless I am not ashamed: **for I know whom I have believed**, and am persuaded that He is able to guard my deposit against that day. (2 Timothy 1:12 EDNT)

8. For once your heart was in darkness, but now it is filled with light from the Lord: **behave as the product of light: 9. (for the product of light is seen in all goodness, righteousness, and sincerity;) 10. be living proof of what is well-pleasing to the Lord.** (Ephesians 5: 8-10 EDNT)

Look, Pilgrims are landing where angels are standing
on harbors of transparent gold,
The beauties of glory surpass every story
that mortal has dreamed of or told:
What joy and what rapture as heaven we capture
by sailing through stormiest gale.
They feared not the riding for God's hand was guiding,
and His breath was fanning the sails.
Such consolation makes our rough sailing bearable
just to know that God will see us through.

— R. P. Johnson

CHAPTER TEN

Anticipating the Journey's End

By dawn the gale had dwindled into flaw,
A glorious morning followed: with my friend
I climbed the fo'c's'le-head to see; we saw
The waters hurrying shoreward without end.

From The Wanderer by John Masefield's "Seafaring poetry"

"Land, Ho!"

After a long voyage a sailor has three opportunities to celebrate the end of the Journey: 1) The night before he can see the lights of the approaching harbor. 2) The morning of arrival with the first sight of land and he hears "Land, Ho!" and rejoices that the long journey is nearly over. 3) As the ship docks in a safe harbor and the sailor knows for sure the journey was successful, he rejoices in a secure and safe place to stand. A sailor after a long sea voyage may even kiss the ground in celebration of arrival in port. What will it be like when the Ship of Zion docks and we finally step on to the shores of Heaven? The end will be worth the struggles of the journey. Paul rejoiced in anticipation of heaven:

Since we are children, then heirs, and fellow-heirs with Christ; if we suffer together we may also be glorified together. For I consider the sufferings we now endure not worthy to be compared with the glory about to be revealed in us. (Romans 8:17, 18 EDNT)

The words of the song, *Glorious Day* clearly tell the story of the sacrifice of Jesus and the power of the resurrection that guarantees the He will safely pilot the Ship of Zion and all aboard to the safe harbor of Heaven.   Arrival in port will be a Glorious Day:

GLORIOUS DAY
(Living He Loved Me)

By John Mark Hall and Michael Bleecker

(Chorus)

Living He loved me, dying He saved me
Buried He carried my sins far away
Rising He justified freely forever
One day He's coming, oh, glorious day!

One day when Heaven was filled with His praises
One day when sin was as black as could be
Jesus came forth to be born of a Virgin
Dwelt among men, my example is He.

One day they led Him up Calvary's mountain
One day they nailed Him to die on a tree
Suffering anguish, despised and rejected
Bearing our sins, my Redeemer is He.

One day the grave could conceal Him no longer
One day the stone rolled away from the door
Then He arose, over death He had conquered
Now He's ascended, my Lord evermore.

One day the trumpet will sound for His coming
One day the skies with His glories will shine

Wonderful day, my beloved one bringing
My Savior, Jesus is mine!

Permanent Housing in Heaven

1. For we know that when our earthly tent is dismantled, we have an eternal heavenly building from God not made with hands. 2. Because of this we cry out desiring earnestly to move into a permanent home in heaven: 3. being permanently housed in heaven, we shall not be found destitute. 4. While in a temporary tent we are burdened with earthly emotion about dying, desiring that mortality would be swallowed up of life. 5. Now God has prepared us for this by giving us the down payment of the Spirit as a guarantee of eternal life. 6. Being therefore always fully assured knowing that while we are present in the body, we are absent from the Lord: 7. (For we walk by faith, not by vision): 8. I repeat, we are full of assurance and willing to be absent from the body to be present with the Lord. 9. Wherefore, we devote ourselves zealously to please the Lord whether at home or absent. 10. The sum total of us must appear before the judgment seat of Christ; that the whole character of every one may be made manifest to receive a recompense for things done in the body whether good or worthless. (2 Corinthians 5:1-10 EDNT)

There is no place in scripture where an unconverted person is required or invited to a public building to find salvation. New Testament soul winning was a daily lifestyle in both the home and the marketplace. One found his brother. Another found a friend. A woman at a well witnessed about Jesus and a whole city came and believed because of her testimony and words of Jesus.

The death of Stephen initiated the conversion of Saul of Tarsus. When he delayed, God's light intervened and Saul was sent to the Straight Street home of a believer for prayer and guidance. His conversion took place in a private house not a public place of worship. This informs the current need of Christianity: the homes of believers should be a place of family worship, personal witness and regular evangelism.

Perhaps this is the missing element in the advancement of the gospel.

Evangelism is reaching people at their point of need at the earliest point in time at the greatest distance from a house of worship. The commission of early followers of Jesus was to make disciples as they traveled around the known world. With modern travel and technology, evangelism should be effective through the personal witness. Reaching individuals as early as possible and then bringing them together with other believers for learning and growing in grace is the New Testament model.

A Change of Heart That Leads to Life

1. The apostles and brethren in all Judaea heard that the Gentiles had also received the word of God. 2. And when Peter returned to Jerusalem, the stricter Jews took issue with him, 3. saying, You visited and ate with men who were not Jews. 4. But Peter explained the facts from the beginning, saying, 5. I was praying in the city of Joppa and fell into a trance and saw heaven open and something like a sheet of sail-cloth being let down to earth by ropes at the four corners: 6. It contained all manner of four-footed beasts and creeping and flying things. 7. And a voice said, Rise, Peter; kill and eat. 8. But I said, Not so, Lord; for I have never eaten anything that is unholy. 9. And the voice spoke again, What God had cleansed, you must not call defiled. 10. This happened three times and suddenly it all disappeared into heaven. 11. Immediately there were three men already come where I was, sent from Caesarea to me. 12. And the Spirit told me to go with them, nothing doubting. Moreover these six brethren accompanied me, and we entered into the man's house: 13. And he told us how he had seen an Angel in his house, which stood and said, Send men to Joppa, and call for Simon, whose surname is Peter; 14. who shall tell you words, whereby you and your house will be saved. 15. And as I began to speak, the Holy Spirit fell on them, just as He did on us originally. 16. Then I remembered the word of the Lord, how He said, John indeed baptized with water; but you shall be baptized with the Holy Spirit. 17. Now since God

granted to them the same gift He gave us, when we believed on the Lord Jesus Christ; who was I, that I could resist God? 18. On hearing this, they were silenced and praised God, saying, God has also granted the Gentiles a change of heart that leads to life. (Acts 11:1-18 EDNT)

As attendance declined, the state sponsored churches of England were dying a slow and painful death. Booth in explaining his Salvation Army shared the church may ring bells rings that sound out, "Come to church, come to church" but the lost do not come. My army of believers goes to the streets and beats a base drum that says, "Fetch um! Fetch um! And we get them!" This was meeting the challenge and using opportunity to take the message to the streets. Basic soul winning is reaching the lost in the market place where they live and work. Booth understood this fact, and his Salvation Army practiced what he preached.

The Salvation Army

Booth's Army of believers would station themselves and their band outside a busy Pub and play popular tunes. When the music filtered into the Pub, men would gather to hear the music and Booth's Salvation Army Band would put Christian words to the popular tunes and got the message of grace and salvation to the lost, the lonely, and the forgotten. Booth successfully navigated the challenges of faith-based behavior.

The stained glass of the church often becomes a barrier and hinders the poor who would gladly hear the good news about Jesus. Without proper clothing or an understanding of God's redemption plan, the lost refuse to enter the sacred sanctuary of the saints. Yet, the saints could reach them in the streets, but prefer to sit on the premises of their sanctuary and sing "Standing on the Promises" without listening to the words of the song. Perhaps they should remember the Word clearly records responsibility for idle words.

36. But I say, for every useless expression that men shall speak, they will give account in the Day of Judgment. 37. For by your words you shall be acquitted, and by your words you shall be condemned. (Matthew 12:36-37 EDNT)

Spiritual Discipline

Some faith-based groups have become a "club for sinners" and a "hospital for sleeping saints" who attend service to soothe their conscience and pretend to serve God. What would happen if the Holy Spirit maintained the same spiritual discipline as that dealt with Ananias and Sapphira (Acts 5:1-12) who permitted Satan to influence their heart to lie to the Holy Spirit? Living a lie is as bad as telling a lie. What would happen to the present congregation when their behavior does not match their profession?

Lifestyle of the rich and famous who seem to get the most they can out of life is similar to the conduct of supposed saints who participate in religious activities to advance themselves rather than to serve God. While the poor, the homeless remain lost in the streets, weak followers continue to "sing and play church." This is the circumstance of those who refuse to completely follow Jesus because they fear the true lifestyle and hardships of those who follower Christ. They take the easy way by slipping into a service and slipping out unchanged. The Christian life is not a bed of roses, but has struggles and difficulties. All humans have a short life filled with troubles (Job 14:1); therefore, why should one expect a life of ease as a Christian.

Early believers had difficulties that present day believers could never understand or endure. The early disciples acted boldly with courage and spoke fluently of God's redemption in the midst of suffering and persecution. They remained strong in faith with the support of the Holy Spirit and the fellowship of other believers. Modern believers in the West have not suffered the same privations and persecutions as some present day believers who live in other parts of the world. For example, a pastor in Iran was sentenced to death simply because he converted from Islam to Christianity. According to Hebrews 12:4, modern believers may struggle against sin and evil, but they have not yet been tortured and put to death for their faith. We are asked to develop the lifestyle of a martyr whose existence is a witness to God's saving grace.

Paul struggled to take the Gospel to the lost, yet he clearly understood that the sufferings of the present were not worthy to be compared with God's blessings and the glory that would be revealed when one's lifestyle brings hope and salvation to the lost (Romans 8:18). When we see the struggle of early believers, the present difficulties in witnessing and sharing the Gospel are diminished. The stories of the heroes of faith should provide courage to pursue a lifestyle of faith and behavior that pleases God and leads other to hope and redemption. David was a king without a throne, but he did the impossible to save his people from slavery. What can you do to fill a need in your family, community, or place of worship?

40. For us, God had something better in store. **We were needed, to make the history of their lives complete.** (Hebrews 11:32-40 EDNT)

The last phase of that passage of scripture, "We were needed, to make the history of their lives complete" speaks volumes to the lethargic and weak witness exhibited by so many professing Christians. Paul wrote about these issues in Romans:

1. I implore you, brethren, by the compassions of God that you place yourselves as a living sacrifice, consecrated and pleasing to God, which is your reasonable worship. 2. And be not fashioned according to this age: but be transformed by a new mental attitude, that you may confirm for yourselves what is good, acceptable, and the complete will of God. 3. For I say this through the grace given unto me, to every man that is among you, not to be high-minded more than he ought to be minded; but to be sober-minded, according to the measure of faith

God has given. 4. For as the human body has many parts, and all parts do not have the same function: 5. so we, being many form one body in Christ, and each one is mutually dependent on another. 6. Having gifts that differ according to the grace given to us; if your gift is inspired speech, practice according to your proportion of faith; 7. If your gift is serving others, minister well: and the teacher concentrate on teaching; 8. the one who exhorts, must give attention to consolation; he who gives food, clothing or shelter for the poor, let it be done with no partiality; he that governs must do it with diligence; the one who shows compassion must do it with cheerfulness. (Romans 12:1-8 EDNT)

The Lower Lights

During the seafaring era, individuals along the coast had the responsibility of preparing signal fires along the shore. During a storm, they would start the fires as a signal to sailors in the water. When a sailor has to abandon a sinking ship at night or in a high-wave storm, it is difficult to know the way to shore. Sailors in the water could see light from the fires and know which way to swim toward the shore. Such fires became known as "The Lower Lights."

One of the great gospel songs that some may remember from their childhood is *Let the Lower Lights Be Burning*. Many understood the song even before they saw a lighthouse. The song was written by a talented young musician, Philip P. Bliss, (1871). While traveling with Dwight L. Moody, Bliss was impressed by an illustration about a violent storm on Lake Erie that was often repeated in a Moody sermon.

It seems that on a dark and stormy night, when the waves rolled like mountains with no star to be seen, a ship, rocking and plunging, neared the harbor. "Are you sure this is the right harbor," asked the Captain, seeing only light from the lighthouse? "Quite sure, sir," replied the pilot. "Where are the lower lights" asked the Captain? "Gone out, sir!" was the answer. "Can you make the harbor?" "We must, or perish, sir."

With a strong hand and a brave heart, the pilot turned the wheel, but in the darkness, he missed the channel, and the ship crashed on the rocks. The ship was lost and many sailors had a watery grave. Moody would conclude his powerful sermon, "Brethren, the Master will take care of the great lighthouse. Let us keep the lower lights burning."

Brightly beams our Father's mercy from His lighthouse evermore,
But to us He gives the keeping of the lights along the shore.
Let the lower lights be burning! Send a gleam across the wave!
Some poor struggling, fainting seaman you may rescue,
you may save.

Dark the night of sin has settled, loud the angry billows roar;
Eager eyes are watching, longing, for the lights, along the shore.
Let the lower lights be burning! Send a gleam across the wave!
Eager eyes are watching, longing, for the lights, along the shore.

— Philip P. Bliss (1871)

The Garbage Can Witness

Questioning an elderly man about the process of handing out Gospel tracts in a fast food location, many of which would end in the garbage, was asked about the process. "How do you feel about people taking a tract and then discarding it in the trash?" His response was informative and mature, "My task is to witness, the Holy Spirit deals with the tract after it leaves my hand. Some may end up in the trash, but even in that, God has a plan. Maybe some down and out individual going through the garbage searching for something of value will find the tract and be prompted to receive Christ." Then the man took advantage of an interested person and presented a 1, 2, 3 plan to salvation:

There is only one Way to God - through Jesus!

For God so loved the world, that He gave His only begotten Son, that whosoever believeth in Him should not perish, but have everlasting life (John 3:16)

I am the door, by Me if any man enter in, he shall be saved, and shall go in and out, and find pasture. (John 10:9)

Jesus saith unto him, I am the Way, the Truth, and the Life, no man cometh unto the Father, but by Me. (John 14:6)

Neither is there salvation in any other: for there is none other Name under heaven given among men, whereby we must be saved. (Acts 4:12)

Salvation is by grace alone!

For by grace are ye saved through faith: and that not of yourselves: it is the gift of God: Not of works, lest any man should boast. (Ephesians 2:8-9)

But we believe that through the grace of the Lord Jesus Christ we shall be saved, even as they. (Acts 15:11)

Being justified freely by His grace through the redemption that is in Christ Jesus: (Romans 3:24)

In whom we have redemption through His blood, the forgiveness of sins, according to the riches of His grace. (Ephesians 1:7)

Salvation can be yours now!

But as many as received Him, to them gave He power to become the sons of God, even to them that believe on His name. (John 1:12)

For whosoever shall call upon the Name of the Lord shall be saved. (Luke 13:3)

Afterword

Life, as a journey, is deeply embedded in all cultures and in all times. Indeed in some cultures, the afterlife is also regarded as a journey. It would seem self evident, therefore, that to ensure a safe and fulfilling voyage, we need to embrace the highest and most effective strategies. Indeed we are not lacking in strategies for the Journey of Life. We are awash with ideas from Lucretius, the Greek philosopher to Dr. Phil (the current television guru) on avoiding the hazards on the journey of life and how to live life well. Most of these strategies fail because they do not reflect the core issue at our psyche, viz, the need in life for a deep and abiding relationship to quench the void we all feel. This book by Subesh Ramjattan is about such a relationship.

Further the book recognizes our need not only for a deep and abiding relationship, but for someone to hold our hands and guide us as we journey through life. Regardless of one's worldview or belief system, the incontrovertible fact of life is that none of us has a map, or even know our final destination. It is also an incontrovertible fact, as Woody Allen said, "No one gets out of life alive." Death, then is the last event of this life, but is that our destination? Subesh Ramjattan presents a book framed within a nautical analogy, emphasizing the foundational principles of Christianity, specifically that our destination is Heaven, that this life is merely a preparation for that, and death is merely a transition. The author states the purpose of his book is to "encourage my friends to make a faith-based commitment and scriptural connection with Jesus and other believers. The seafaring theme was to assist both the faith and behaviour of those who would follow Christ." The author throughout anchors his ideas on biblical references avoiding a major pitfall of books on lifestyle issues, that is the risk of self knowing, a symptom of the hubris we carry from the beginning of time. I commend this book to all Christians and to anyone seeking a basis for living a truly moral life.

— **Emmanuel Persad,** M.B.B.S; Dip .Psy; F.R.C.P; D.F.C.P.A
Professor Emeritus, Western University, Ontario, Canada
Professor, Queen's University, Ontario, Canada.
Professor, Northern Ontario School of Medicine, Ontario, Canada

About the Author

Subesh Ramjattan is a remarkable man who is hungry for knowledge and reaches for every kernel of truth he can find from any source. His life journey began in a poor village learning common-sense lessons from his family and the village environment. He proceeded to learn more in school and as a young man working hard to gather both the knowledge and the resources needed to start his own business. He listens to anyone who speaks and reads everything in sight. Subesh remembers almost everything good he hears, sees, or learns from any source. He is unselfish in giving resources for projects for the disadvantaged and constantly demonstrates his concern for faith-based operations and the individual believers who take an active role in faith-based groups.

Subesh is a serious student of all subjects that touch his life, business and spiritual commitment. When he discovers the interrelationship of concepts and constructs, he desires to share them with others. This interest has resulted in a business and spiritual journey that has increased the quality of life for many. His first book, *The Anapausis Partnership*, co-authored with his wife, Debra, catalogued much of the business and spiritual journey that established a model of philanthropy, mentoring, and coaching to improve the quality of life for the disadvantaged of Trinidad and Tobago. The documentation of this process produced the awarding of a Doctor of Humane Letters (DHL) by OASIS University's Institute of Higher Learning.

Dr. Ramjattan's second book, *God's Work Done God's Way*, reveals more of his character and passion for believers and the disadvantaged. His third book, *Living a Life Larger than Yourself*, speaks to the quality of life he desires for all of God's children from the cradle to the grave. This book, *Navigating the Challenges of Faith-based Behavior,* is a sincere effort to reach family, friends and colleagues with the values and lifestyle that reflects the impact of

God in life and living. Perhaps the most meaningful aspect of the life of Subesh and Debra Ramjattan, is that they give all the credit to God for their blessings and their ability to bless others.

Dr. Ramjattan's years of service were recognized by several international organizations:

- The International Third World Leaders Association awarded him the KINGDOM STATESMAN AWARD for 2011. This award was given for leadership which demonstrated maturity, quality and character as a Statesman and more than 30-years of distinguished service.

- HUMANeX VENTURES honored him as a COMMUNITY EXEMPLAR in 2013. A Community Exemplar is highlighted by a life of significant impact, multiplied through thousands of those that they impact directly and indirectly, in ways that will live beyond the present and be felt, modeled, and multiplied for many, many years---a rich legacy for generations. According to HUMANeX VENTURES those who receive this award are:
  - Craftsmen of their trade
  - Passionate to teach and lead
  - Motivators
  - Role models of Excellence
  - Innovators
  - Creators of meaning their lives and the lives of others
  - Dream makers
  - Catalysts in making a difference
  - Developers of talent and potential
  - Listeners
  - High achievers that impact the lives of any
  - Multipliers
  - Activators of change
  - Educators

- Masters with a purpose
- Influencers
- Doers and Dreamers
- Impact and Legacy Builders.

- Global Educational Advance, Inc. admitted Dr. Ramjattan with all rights and privileges to the ORDER OF MEPHIBOSHETH on July 27, 2013, recognizing his understanding that each child is different and honoring his faithful following of faith-based principles and unselfish investing of resources and energy to build bridges of hope and care for disadvantaged children.

Reference and Reading List

Borthwick, Paul. (2003) *Stop Witnessing and Start Loving*. NavPress.

Bonhoeffer, Dietrich (1985) *Spiritual Care*. Minneapolis: Fortress Press.

Chambers, Oswald. (reprint) *My Utmost for His Highest*. Foundation.

Coleman, Robert E. (2000) *The Master Plan of Evangelism*. Spire.

Craig, G. Bartholomew and Michael Goheen, (2002) *Finding Our Place in the Biblical Story*. Grand Rapids: Baker.

Dallas, Willard, (2002) *Renovation of the Heart: Putting on the Character of Christ*. Colorado Springs: NavPress.

Dunagin, Richard L. (1999) *Beyond These Walls*. Nashville: Abingdon Press.

Eisenman, Tom. (1987) *Everyday Evangelism – Making the Most of Life's Common Moments*. Grand Rapids: IVP

Foster, Richard (1978) *The Celebration of Discipline: The Path to Spiritual Growth*. San Francisco: HarperCollins.

Foxe, John, (2009) *Foxe's Book of Martyrs: Select Narratives*. Oxford University Press.

Green, Hollis L. (2007) *Discipleship*. Nashville: GlobalEdAdvance Press.

Green, Hollis L. (2007) *Why Churches Die*, Nashville: GlobalEdAdvance Press.

Green, Hollis L. (2012) *The EVERGREEN Devotional New Testament -- Complete Edition*, Nashville: GlobalEdAdvancePress.

Green, Michael, ed. (2002) *Church Without Walls: A Global Examination of the Cell Church*. Grand Rapids: Eerdmans.

Green, Michael. (1970) *Evangelism in the Early Church*. Grand Rapids; Eerdmans.

Harding, Kevass J. (2007) *Can These Bones Live?: Bringing New Life to a Dying Church*. Nashville: Abingdon Press.

Hybels, Bill. (2006) *Just Walk Across The Room: Simple Steps to Pointing People to Faith*. Grand Rapids: Zondervan.

Little, Paul. (1988) *How to Give Away Your Faith*. Grand Rapids: IVP

Mittleberg, Mark. (2008) *Choosing Your Faith: In a World of Spiritual Options*. Tyndale House Publishers.

Moore, R. York. (2005) *Growing Your Faith by Giving it Away*. Grand Rapids: IVP

Osbeck, K. W. (1985). *101 more hymn stories*. Grand Rapids, Mich.: Kregel Publications

Ramjattan, Subesh and Debra. (2011) T*he Anapausis Partnership*. Nashville: GlobalEdAdvancePress.

Ramjattan, Subesh (2012) *God's Work Done God's Way*. Nashville: GlobalEdAdvancePress.

Ramjattan, Subesh (2012) *Living a Life LARGER than Yourself*. Nashville: GlobalEdAdvancePress.

Staniforth, Maxwell. (1989) trans. *Early Christian Writings*. London: Penguin Books.

Sorenson, Stephen. (2005) *Like Your Neighbor?: Doing Everyday Evangelism on Common Ground*. Grand Rapids: IVP.

Titelman, Gregory Y. (1996), *Random House Dictionary of Popular Proverbs and Sayings*, Random House.

Wagner, C. Peter. (2006) *The Church in the Workplace: How God's People Can Transform Society*. Ventura, CA: Regal.

Weil, Louis (1986) *Gathered to Pray: Understanding Liturgical Prayer*. Cambridge, MA: Crowley Publications.

Wisdom From Mother Teresa

People are often unreasonable and self-centered.
Forgive them anyway.

If you are kind, people may accuse you of ulterior motives.
Be kind anyway.

If you are honest, people may cheat you.
Be honest anyway.

If you find happiness, people may be jealous.
Be happy anyway.

The Good you do today may be forgotten tomorrow.
Do good anyway.

Give the world the best you have and it may never be enough.
Give your best anyway.

For you see, in the end, it is between you and God.

It was never between you and them anyway.

www.ingramcontent.com/pod-product-compliance
Lightning Source LLC
Chambersburg PA
CBHW021109090426
42738CB00006B/571